# Education and Politics:
## Policy-Making in Local Education Authorities

## ROBERT E. JENNINGS

*State University of New York at Buffalo*

B. T. Batsford Ltd
London

First published 1977
© Robert E. Jennings 1977

ISBN 0 7134 0474 4 (Hardcover edition)
ISBN 0 7134 0475 2 (Limp edition)

Filmset in 11 on 12pt Plantin
by Weatherby Woolnough, Sanders Road,
Wellingborough, Northamptonshire
Printed by Billing & Son Ltd,
London, Guildford and Worcester
for the publishers B. T. Batsford Ltd,
4 Fitzhardinge Street, London W1H 0AH

# Contents

# Acknowledgments

I want to express my appreciation to the councillors and officers of the six authorities, not only for sharing their perceptions and understandings of local government but also for their generous hospitality. Sabbatical support by my department at Buffalo made the study possible and Professor G. N. Brown, Director of the Institute of Education, University of Keele, provided the facilitating services essential to a visiting researcher. Mr A. K. C. Campbell, Tutor Librarian, aided me in locating the relevant literature, while colleagues at several universities and polytechnics shared the findings of their ongoing projects. My thanks are also due to Graham Higgins and John Eggleston at Keele and Mike Milstein at Buffalo for reading and criticizing the manuscript. Ellen Kalway typed the drafts, diligently learning British spellings and forms.

Robert E. Jennings
Eggertsville, New York
August 1976

# Foreword

*Professor John Eggleston, University of Keele*

One of the enduring pieces of western folk wisdom is the adage that the outsider sees more of the game. It is an adage that had been translated into the impeccable scientific respectability of the concept of the detached social scientist who, never having lived the life of his subjects and yet never free from emotional entanglement with them, is able to diagnose their behaviour and motivations with surgical objectivity. Yet this is a position that has been under widespread challenge from sociologists who claim that detachment can lead to insensitivity and therefore to ignorance. Amongst others, Becker in his notable work *The Outsider* has suggested that, only when one has painfully and successfully come to know and use the complex subtleties of shared meaning within a human group oneself, can one begin to understand the behaviour that is taking place.

When the behaviour under observation happens to be the process of politics and policy-making in English local education authorities—processes that are complex, subtle and only partially visible—and when the observer is an American educationalist whose familiarity is predominantly with systems of educational administration that are fundamentally different in nature, the following question inevitably arises, 'Can the study give rise to new insights that are of real value to the insiders?' In his study, Dr Jennings has impressively demonstrated that it can, and his achievement springs from a skilful combination of roles. He has assiduously studied the interwoven threads of decision-making in six English local education authorities, noticing previously unrecognized connections, probing dark corners and amassing a well-organized and illuminating selection of evidence by adopting the 'detached social scientist' approach. However, he has gone on from there in a equally skilful manner to establish himself as an insider, sensitive to the subtleties and nuances of the world of the local education authority, its politicians and administrators. The juxtaposition of these approaches has led Dr Jennings to a highly illuminative perspective which is made even more useful by his capacity to add, on appropriate occasions, a comparative dimension to his analyses of policy and practice.

In his analyses Dr Jennings teases out the central nature of the party political control of education and the crucial way this acts through the committee structure. He deals with the marginal but often focal 'non-political' roles, coopted members, school governors, teachers' representatives and the pressure and interest groups that have inserted themselves into the official machine. He considers the way in which these marginal roles are achieved and often are taken over or at least are controlled in turn by the party system. He looks at the components for effective participation in decision-making, information, personnel, finance and influence. He considers the ways in which the various administrative processes are at one moment visible and public, at another insulated and private. He emphasizes the paradox of an educational system that, though committed to increasing flexibility in its schools, finds itself increasingly rigid and inflexible in its administrative devices. He draws attention in a way that already seems prophetic to the continuing magnitude of the financial problems of education and to the way in which these translate the education service into an area of major national as well as political controversy, intensifying the already dominant political characteristics of educational decision-making. Here Dr Jennings' typology of the political characteristics and strategies of local education authorities is of particular value and allows him to ask and answer some previously unaskable questions such as: 'What difference does it make which party is in power?'

Perhaps the major contribution of the book lies in its consideration of the ways in which the professional administrators, notably the chief education officers, relate to the party politicians, the complex paths of consultation that link them and the subtle ways in which power comes to be shared between the professionals and the politicians. Here Dr Jennings has taken us in detail to the heart of the English educational system. His book is a timely document at a time when the system is in flux with changing local boundaries, with new and lower predictions of school populations and with continuing major reorganizations taking place in the secondary schools and in tertiary education. Teachers, students, parents, politicians and administrators will appreciate Dr Jennings' energy and will find valuable information and understanding in his analyses.

# Introduction

Politics and policy-making are a useful mix. The labyrinth of political and administrative decisions of which the policy process is made, the various control mechanisms of party and government and the interplay of the participants in the process provide a means for defining and solving complex societal problems. However, when the process is applied to an area of endeavour such as education in local authorities where politics, by tradition, are not supposed to intrude and where administrative decisions are expected to reflect only that which is good for children, a fair amount of suspicion arises about its usefulness. If it is realized that most people have two prolonged contacts with schooling, their own and that of their youngsters, it is amazing that there is so much suspicion and so little knowledge about the process by which provision is made for education. A more amazing fact, however, is that many educators and administrators have the same suspicions and little better understanding than laymen. This is slowly being remedied by recent studies, and educators are coming to realize that the disentanglement of education from politics is not likely. Indeed, the trend is in the opposite direction. This realization is bringing about a greater desire to gain more understanding of politics and policy process.

The intent of this book is to help educators, administrators and others to develop their understanding of what is often called the politics of education. Through exploring the political and administrative decision-taking at each of the several stages of the policy process in local authorities and through inquiring into the decisions about how to handle a question or an issue and how to arrive at a solution or spell out an intention, much of what happens can be explained. The intent will be fulfilled if educators can define more clearly their own roles and their relationships to others in the making of policy.There is a bias to the book, however; it is that politics and policy-making are fascinating subjects.

The book is based on research conducted in three Outer London boroughs and three counties in England during 1973-4. The political make-up and control, as well as other characteristics of these authorities, may be briefly described as follows: of the three Outer London boroughs, one is largely suburban dotted with numerous village centres which extend into one another. Politically, it is, as a colleague noted, 'a hotbed of staid Toryism' and the Conservatives usually enjoy a 50-seat majority over Labour in the council. Beginning in 1968, 3 Liberals have also been returned. The second borough authority is divided territorially between a diversified urban area, undergoing redevelopment, and suburban villages with housing estates. The Conservatives control the council, but Labour came within 10 seats of taking over in 1971. In May 1974 they lost several seats, and Conservative control tightened. The third authority is suburban and urban industrial. Labour has been in control by about 12 seats since 1971, following a rout in 1968 when they had been reduced to only 5 seats on the council. The Conservatives regained several seats in 1974, but Labour retained control. Of the three county authorities, one was predominantly urban until the 1974 reorganization balanced its populations between boroughs and rural areas. Until the shadow elections of 1973, the county was dominated by countryside Conservatives and Independents in coalition. After the elections, the Conservatives had a majority of 3 over Labour and organized the council. In addition, there are 1 Liberal and 4 Independent members. The second authority is predominantly rural but contains one large conurbation and several towns. Geographically, this county was unaffected by reorganization except for some boundary straightening. Until 1973 the Conservatives with allied antisocialist Independent support held control, but in the election Labour came to power for the first time in 16 years. Its majority on the council is 8 seats. The third county is rural, and its boundaries were 'not changed by reorganization. The council was Independent-dominated and quite apolitical, but control was taken by an Independent-Conservative coalition following the

1973 elections. Labour counts 18 members including 5 Independents. There are also 4 Liberals on the council.

The methodology is based on a behavioural approach to the study of social and organizational processes. Owing to its exploratory nature and the limitations inherent in being a foreign observer, the approach was made less narrow than is usual. A review of the literature, including previous studies in four of the authorities, was made to develop a background of information and ideas. In each authority, through informal conversations with chief education officers and party leaders, initial identification was made of officials to be interviewed. Those people were selected who were thought to be knowledgeable about education provision and/or local government operation. As the interviews progressed, respondents identified other individuals with a special knowledge of party politics, local organizations and related topics. These people were also interviewed. The interview schedules were designed to obtain respondents' perceptions of the decision processes in the local council, its committees and the education department. Questions were included about the respondents' roles and the roles of others, the party political influences and the constraints affecting local policy-making in education. Each interview took approximately two hours to complete and 90 interviews were held. The respondents were as follows: 33 officers including chief education officers, their deputies and other principal officers, chief executives and their assistants; 46 councillors including leaders of each party in council, chairmen of education committees and subcommittees, shadow chairmen or spokesmen for other parties, finance committee chairmen and other councillors considered influential or as possessing special knowledge useful to the study; 11 others including school governors, coopted members of education committees, teachers' organization officials and leaders of community associations.

In addition to the structured parts of the research, other activities were used to broaden the background and to add further dimensions to the findings. These included informal conversations with academic colleagues in education, government and politics, with several Department of Education and Science officials, with members of local government and education study groups, with teachers and heads of schools and with other observers of the political and educational scene in England such

*3*

as newspaper reporters and editors. Various meetings were attended including council, education and policy committee sessions, department staff meetings and party groups. Some time was also spent in working men's clubs, local Conservative Party parlours and during the May 1974 London elections, two major party candidates were accompanied by the writer as they canvassed their wards.

The plan of the book is as follows. Chapter 1 poses the problem and presents an encapsulated view of the changing national context for local policy-making in education. Policy and its functions in local government are examined in chapter 2. This is followed by a six-stage model of the policy process. The purpose of the model is to provide a framework for categorizing and examining various elements, participants and activities in educational policy-making. In chapter 3, policy-making is placed in its political setting as described in the literature and as perceived by local officials. Chapter 4 looks at constraints on the process, local environments for education, governmental structures and controls on information. How they affect political control and how political control is maintained through them are topics for discussion. Chapter 5 is focused on the participants in the policy process including party leaders in the council, party groups, committee chairmen and officers. Their activities and interrelated roles are detailed and explained from their own perceptions. In chapter 6, these results are brought together and are compared with the model. In chapter 7, conclusions are drawn about the policy process and the politics of education in local authorities, and some predictions are made about the future.

# 1  Education in Politics

When questions about education are being discussed, someone usually observes that everything will be all right if the politicians will keep out of the issue. However, when solutions are proposed, they very often include requests or demands for governmental action. If people are dissatisfied with some aspect of schooling, they often turn on local officials as a contributory cause of the problem. As debates over remedies go on, people complain that the issue has become a political football and that the government is not doing its job effectively. In some instances, when a new policy is announced to meet an emerging situation, either by the central government or by a local council, it is denounced as a political decision rather than as an educational one. These are all reflections of suspicion and concern about the processes by which choices are made in providing for education. They also demonstrate peoples' uncertainty about who is making what decisions in educational matters and where those decisions are being made. The sticking point in these concerns seems to be the nature and extent of political involvement in educational questions, the application of political processes to policy-making for education.

This uncertainty and these concerns do not indicate a total dissatisfaction with the way in which choices are made. Discussion and debate of social questions such as education poses in a democratic system are essential to the making of a policy. Deciding on solutions and allocating societal resources to implement those decisions are also essential if policy-making is to have meaning and effect. Deciding and allocating are functions of government. What is to be debated and put up for decision is the concern of a responsive and responsible citizenry. While there is a general understanding that the political process is the link between societal concern and governmental action, what apparently provokes people is a breakdown between the questions raised and the decisions taken. People feel that issues become politically polarized too early or that proposals for change do not get full consideration owing to political manoeuvring. Indeed, it often appears that the politicians propose and then, after little debate, dispose.

The frustration with educational questions and the manner in which they are decided is particularly aggravating in local education authorities (LEAs). Alternate tacks by central government are not unexpected as political conditions or party control change, and parliamentary juggling of national resources and needs has been going on since the Second World War as Britain has tried to keep its economic balance. However, in local authorities where there has been somewhat of a tradition of non-party or at least non-partisan politics and relatively little manoeuvring room with resources, a similar procedure does not seem necessary or desirable. Furthermore, in many areas of governmental endeavour there is supposedly little that a local council can do but follow central government policies and directives. Thus, when debate on educational matters turns into a slanging match between local officials and the community, many people are surprised and angered to find how much education is tangled in local political processes. Petitions or delegations to the education committee or council from community organizations seem to have no impact. Pertinent questions receive little notice or go unanswered. What may have seemed a mildly controversial item about schools is suddenly spirited away for party group decision, and the whip is put on in the education committee. Some council members are equally surprised to find themselves embroiled in head-on battles with a rate-payers' or parents' association on topics which have curiously become party matters rather than matters to be handled through discussion and consultation at an administrative level or in the council.

Then, too, questions are raised about education on which community-wide discussion seems desirable but which never see the light of day outside the county or borough hall. Political and administrative decisions are made and announced as policy with discussion which is apparently confined to the education department directorate and the education committee led by the chief education officer and the committee chairman. Consultation with other parties-at-interest is minimal or absent. Even the attitude of the council meeting seems like a rubber stamp, approving the committee's action without debate. The process by which decisions were taken remains a mystery except to those people immediately involved. Those who feel left out of the discussion and decision-taking call it politics as usual.

## Politics and Policy: What is the Mix?

In some ways the policy-making process for education at the local level is like a river which disappears in desert sands only to reappear in another place. What has happened between the two points is difficult to determine without some digging. Similarly, the political and administrative decision-making which is educational policy-making needs investigation if there is to be an understanding of what happens to questions about education and provision for education inside local government. There are civics text prescriptions or descriptions of how the process should be conducted, but these do not seem to be very useful as programme cards with which to follow the action. Studies of policy-making in local education, particularly in the period 1965–75, tend to be focused on secondary school reorganization crises and the interaction of community organizations, education committees and chief education officers as they devised policies for going (or not going) comprehensive. While these studies provide valuable information about some critical events in evolving a particular policy, they do not (nor were they intended to) present a more general picture of the educational policy process in local authorities.

Many more facets of the policy process or the politics of education in local authorities require investigation before there will be more than a minimal understanding of it. Future predictions about policy outcomes or adjustments of the process to emerging conditions will not be possible with any degree of certainty until there is some further explanation of the relationships between politics, administration and policy.

The purpose of this book is to explore the mix of politics and policy-making for education within local government. The task is to identify and describe the kinds of process decisions that policy-makers face as they consider how to handle any question or issue. The focus is on how these decisions are taken and the roles played by elected members, officers, committees and party groups in taking those decisions. Each of the several stages of the process from question to policy calls for different kinds of decisions, political and administrative. Conditions which bear on these decisions include the political make-up of the council, the committee structure and administrative organization of the authority and the local environment for education. All have implications for the activities of such people as council and party leaders, committee chairmen and the chief education officer in framing and controlling the process. Examination of the activities and interrelated actions of the participants and identification of who makes which decisions should contribute to a better understanding of the political aspects of the policy process.

## A Focus on Local Government

There are critical reasons for gaining a better grasp of educational policy-making at the local level. Certainly those who participate or who would like to participate need to know as much as possible about the process. Apart from that, however, there is the whole question of how the education system is being developed in the light of changing conditions and perceptions about education. What happens in its governance, the mix of policy-making and politics, profoundly affects the shaping of education towards desired or accepted ends. This is particularly important when the decisions being made have a direct impact on the delivery of services, as is certainly the case in local authorities.

The nature of the societal debate about education has shifted from deciding what the structure of the education system will be to sorting out what uses will be made of that system. These are two entirely different questions which may involve rather different forces or which may call for new roles to be played by old forces (Baron, 1965, p. 53). What emerged from a century of expansion and reform was a compromise structure which gained a fairly broad acceptance by both secularists and religionists and which most social and political groupings in the nation felt could be used to provide basic school services for children. What has been emerging in this century, particularly since the Second World War, includes the extension of basic schooling levels to secondary and tertiary education, the revision and expansion of curricula and the addition of school support services to children and youth.

The controversies that surround these major issues are extremely convoluted as they involve such questions as the extension and opening of educational opportunity to greater numbers, the enhancement of life chances, the economic impact of educational provision and the place of parental wishes in determining children's schooling. When the issue of secondary provision, for example, is considered, the old question of tripartite or bipartite was both defended and assailed on the grounds of opportunity and expense. Storms over going comprehensive rage as much around life chances and parental rights as they do around the changing nature of the curriculum. Defenders of the concept are often as vehement about upholding parental choice as are their opponents, but they are poles apart on the efficacy of this type of school in providing for the enhancement of life chances. Divisions over such questions do not follow well-recognized socioeconomic or political groupings in the nation as they did in the nineteenth century. Working-class people have found themselves shoulder to shoulder with upper middle-class leaders in proposing comprehensives, whilst local Labour party members have had to be prodded by party headquarters at Transport House to fight Conservative proposals for going slow in changing a community's schools. Yet, there are authorities where a Conservative majority went to comprehensives quickly and effectively, even though the middle class had organized to 'save the grammar schools'.

A national consensus on any question is difficult to observe or obtain with this diversity of opinion and the relatively unpredictable groupings of interests. Even where the central government acts to force a consensus on a major issue, this cannot control the controversies which inevitably surround it. Determined interests can harness sufficient power to influence local situations. This happened frequently with secondary reorganization, where anticomprehensive organizations allied themselves with party political factions and other community groups. Councils have divided, and members have taken sides in the related controversies, resulting in decisions which held back progress towards the stated national objective. In a similar vein, central government 'stop, go' policies on nursery education over a 12-year period did not prevent local political parties in some authorities from pressing on with the development for such expansion of provision. Nor did the meagreness of central government support programmes for nursery facilities deter officials from presenting elaborate schemes once it was clear that political sentiment was not unfavourable to the concept.

The point which emerges is that controversies about education are increasingly being acted out in each community. What happens in each community is important, because this is what determines the shape of education and the ends to which the system is bent. Debate and decision at the national level does not resolve controversies surrounding an issue. It sets a direction, and, given a vagueness of national consensus, the battleground merely moves to the local level. This raises a second factor in the question of governance, the role of the local education authority as the government at the operating end of the education system.

Little doubt remains that provision for education in England is a governmental responsibility. This began in 1833 with grant aid to schools controlled by voluntary bodies, and it has been firmly established by numerous Acts of Parliament since that time (Baron, 1965, pp. 46-7). The concept of responsibility has been broadened in scope to include extension of educational opportunity, more general financial provision, classification of education units and setting of a school-leaving age as well as establishment of the statutory bases on which the education system is to be operated. Most importantly, Parliament involved general local government in education through the Education Act of 1902 which made local authorities responsible for educational activities within their areas of jurisdiction (Smith, 1971, p. 94). The reforms embodied in the Education Act of 1944 designated the operation of the educational system to local government while reserving for the central government the power to determine national policies and to ensure effective and reasonable exercise over local authority powers and duties.

However, it is not that simple, as these are two different governments which have both shared responsibilities and separate responsibilities in the same area of endeavour, stemming from the same basic laws. They have different powers, too, which are sometimes wielded in concert and sometimes in opposition to each other. Thus, legal prescriptions as to how things operate cannot be assumed to be descriptions of how things operate in practice (Dearlove, 1973, p. 15). This is more than a matter of central government–local government relationships, although that is relevant to the question. For local government, the operation of the educational system is largely a pragmatic matter of initiation and response, negotiation and settlement within the constraints on action found in particular situations. The central government may then be perceived as one potential constraint among several as local authorities carry out their responsibilities for education.

Each authority faces the task of reexamining its responsibilities as each new circular or directive is issued by the central government. It faces the same task when the council is being lobbied by a parents' association that wants changes in educational provision or when the party in control has an idea it wants to pursue. This is necessary before the authority can proceed with determining how it should act (if it should act), with whom it should consult and what the policy result should look like. As might be expected in issues which revolve around the uses of education, new ground is being cultivated, and there is little in the way of national experience against which the authority can compare its possible actions and outcomes.

How the authority should act and whom it should consult may be broadly outlined in law, at least in terms of forms to be followed. How it acts and who it consults in practice are matters largely determined by influence and control within the council and the community. This is where policy-making and politics become mixed. There are decisions which have to be made about the steps to be taken in developing policy, steps which revolve about the roles of officers, members, committee chairmen and council leaders. What these decisions will be depends, in part, on such factors as party political make-up in the council, conventions in the local education authority and local pressures as related to the controversies in the given issue. Such decisions are at the core of the policy process.

There are constraints, too. Each authority must pay attention to the availability of resources and to the numerous community services such as housing and social welfare which compete for those resources. Decisions have to be made for allocating money to education, and, with the end of earmarked funds in the rate support grant, education has to compete more than ever before. These decisions have implications for the rates set by the authority and thus political implications for the process by which policy is made.

The point is that the local authority is a government which has a dynamic of its own. It may not be totally free within the two-tiered system of British government, but it cannot be totally captive. While it has responsibilities to carry out in education, it has, as a government, sufficient autonomy to devise and develop its internal processes for policy-making. What those processes are and how they are conducted affects the policies devised and implemented at the operating end of the educational system.

The decade of the 1970s appears to be providing a changing context for examination of local government processes by which education is shaped. Describing that context is rather like shooting at a moving target as events go forward. Nevertheless, it is necessary to mark out some trends which seem to be propelling the question into greater prominence.

## Context

A series of changes which are taking place on the national scene are showing local decision processes in a new light. These changes are culminations of several long-term movements in the governmental outlook for education, some redefinition of inter-governmental relationships and a rise in the importance of local government. All these changes are giving a new twist to the role of politics in education. First, the central government has apparently lowered the priority of education in its ranking of social matters, and the political parties are less in harmony about what to do in education than they were in the 1960s. Second, the Department of Education and Science seems to be moving from uniformity in regulations towards acceptance of greater variance in local authority needs and capabilities. With this has come increased emphasis on the trend towards cooperation between the two, but the opportunity for political manoeuvring at the local level has also increased, contributing to mistrust between the two. Third, local government as a government and as a political entity has become more important, following its reorganization in 1974. While the redistribution of responsibilities to the new authorities was not great, the tendency was to place broad policy-making and administrative powers at the level most likely to come under party political control. The 'inherent' nature of the political parties has intensified the vying for control in the new authorities. The trends pointing to these contextual changes are introduced here and will be examined in later chapters as they make their impact on various aspects of local policy-making.

*Loss of a Consensus*

In three decades, central government concern for primary and secondary education as a critical social service increased enormously. More and better schooling was a potential curative for social ills which was supported by political parties. This began with the post-war Labour government's determination to fulfil the promises of the 1944 Education Act and its own philosophical bent to disperse the benefits of education throughout the lower end of the socioeconomic spectrum. The Conservatives were not far behind in promoting technical education and in increasing financial support. For nearly 30 years the manifestos and actions of both parties have increasingly stressed what should be done and the benefits to be reaped by investing in education, but other services to people have come into vogue and seem to have a higher priority in the 1970s.

The wave of interest in education probably crested in the 1960s, before secondary reorganization got underway in earnest. At the crest there was the period of a national consensus about education identified by Locke (1974, pp. 3–4). The Conservative and Labour parties tended to find and to help define the mainstream of educational progress. Educational ideas gained, and politics seemed to recede. Greater financial support was given for school facilities and teacher training. Curricular improvement through the Schools Council, examination of the particular needs of pupils, their implications for school organization (by such committees as the Newsom and Plowden Committees) and the raising of the school-leaving age were all established. The problem of immigrant education was faced. Study of the integration of the public schools with the state system was undertaken, and in 1965 the reorganization of secondary education and the elimination of the eleven-plus examinations was started. Both parties put forward, as ministers of education, able men who were determined to improve government provision. Both Sir Edward Boyle, Conservative minister from 1962 to 1964, and Anthony Crosland, Labour minister from 1964 to 1967, characterized their roles as obtaining the most for their department and by championing their service within the government (Kogan, 1971a, p. 38). During these years, too, there was an emphasis on consultation with the many powerful interest groups such as the National Union of Teachers, the Association of Education Committees and the Confederation for the Advancement of State Education (Kogan, 1971b, pp. 44-5). Problems, questions and ideas were exchanged for the purposes of achieving a continued consensus and for keeping the wreckers of both parties at bay.

In this consensus period, the partnership between the central government and the local authority in education seemed to flourish. The ease of communication and the several avenues for achieving harmony reinforced the notion of common interest and common action. Confrontation which could have destroyed the harmony was avoided through patient negotiation of issues and next steps. Where aggravations appeared, interest groups aligned with the consensus entered the negotiation to remind their local memberships where the mainstream was and to outline the reasons for remaining within it. The rationale was simple: the central government can compel compliance but has chosen to proceed on the basis of cooperation; if compulsion comes, local authorities and education will be the losers. It was a time of expansion, and funds were being supplied quite readily. Certainly no one wanted to break up the partnership at the risk of losing money either through ministry disapprovals or even worse through government budget-cutting on the basis of disagreement over the directions which education should take.

However, the consensus did not last owing to a combination of factors which had their cumulative effect at the local level. The Labour government's decision to reorganize secondary education along comprehensive lines and the method for doing so through central-local cooperation provided an opening for those forces which felt their views had not received proper consideration. Supporters of independent schools, the National Association of

School Masters, factions within the National Union of Teachers and some elements in the Conservative Party were among those who felt that a consensus had become a left progressive steamroller. These dissidents had been sharpening their knives before 1965 in such places as Tynemouth (Eccles, 1974), Croydon (Urwin, 1965, pp. 201–29), Corby (Eggleston, 1966) and Bristol (Wood, 1973). Reorganization was often at the core, but related issues including selection, amalgamation, places in fee-paying schools were also argued. When Circular 10/65 was issued requesting local authorities to submit plans for going comprehensive rather than requiring plans, the floodgates were opened for the bitter battles such as took place in Ealing (*Education*, 1972, p. iv), Croydon again and Surrey (Saran, 1973, pp. 18–20, 70).

Local authorities were vulnerable to attack, and what dissident forces could not accomplish at Whitehall they could accomplish at the operating end of the system. If local government decisions could be modified or stalled, the cumulative result might be a national reappraisal of educational policies. Three conventional patterns in handling educational problems were weaknesses exploited by dissidents. In local authorities, education was supposedly a politically neutral area. Community pressure on educational issues, while not unheard of, was not an expected nor fully acceptable means of influencing change. Within the government and within the education service there was usually a tacit agreement to work out differences from within rather than to resort to open argument or to make power plays through alliances with other groups. The impact of the controversies which surrounded the reorganization of secondary education broke in on these conventional patterns. Council members became torn between community desires, as argued by various associations, and party policy as the councillors understood it. Where party influence was weak, other influences often won. Even where the party was strong, some councillors felt that party intrusion into education was wrong, and they deserted the party group on critical issues. Education officers tried to keep various factions working together, but teachers and headmasters took sides with parent groups and others who believed in comprehensives or with those who thought that the end of selection would erode standards. Organizations at the local level received encouragement and help from national interest groups.

Whether pro or con, the message was that the council had to hear their views and that lobbying in education was no longer a dirty word.

By the time the first Black Papers were published in 1969, offering the opinions of dissident academics as a rallying point, the consensus had collapsed. An effective bloc had emerged, opposed to a national policy and resentful of the haste in its implementation. The rise of this bloc forced the two major parties to draw back from a consensus to more traditional stances. The Labour government had reacted earlier by hardening its policy through Circular 10/66 and by firmly tying the approvals of new facilities to acceptable plans for reorganization. It also signalled its determination in 1969 by going to the left in its choice of a new Secretary of State for Education and Science, Edward Short. The Conservatives responded by moving right when they came to power again in 1970. Circular 10/70 was issued, removing from local authorities any obligation to submit reorganization schemes or to proceed with prior plans. Margaret Thatcher, as Secretary of State, enforced this change and, by using the powers under Section 13 of the 1944 Act requiring local education authority submission of requests to alter the character of individual schools, put secondary reorganization on a school-by-school basis.

The central government has since begun to pay more attention to other problems, and education appears to be sliding down the back of the wave. The demand for social welfare provision, the sagging National Health Service, the acute housing shortage and the impact of multiple economic crises seem more critical. All public sector spending for education stabilized in 1971 at 6.2% of the gross national product, after having risen from 4.8% in 1964. By 1973 the schools' share of the education budget was 55.9%. It had peaked at 56.6% in 1965 but dipped to 53.0% in 1969. The relative shrinkage of education as a cause or as an area for top priority attention was especially noticeable in the much-revised 1972 White Paper on the expansion of education (Cmnd. 5174) issued by the Conservative government. Its theme of consolidation and caution in provision belie its title. When the first 1974 Labour government reaffirmed secondary reorganization aims in Circular 4/74, there was little national reaction, indicating a recognition that the remaining struggles would be played out at the local level.

The dissolution of a consensus has left a legacy of changed attitudes about decision-making for education in local government. There is a conviction that local officials can manoeuvre within central government mandates if pressed to do so. This does not mean that pressures have constantly increased; they have not, but the reticence to influence local education authority decisions by lobbying is gone. The political parties have recognized that what was believed to be a politically neutral area was really a fertile field for various interests to promote their views and to create havoc. The reaction has been to delineate party philosophy and policy within the local organization. Party lines have hardened in imitation of, but not in subordination to, the national parties, often with aid from national headquarters. With increased focus on local struggles, parties will not be pre-empted again by leaving the field to others. Education officers have become wary of political factions, community groups and teachers' organizations. Politics and relationships within the service have intruded more and more on their thinking. What could formerly be put forward as sound educational recommendations now have to be given litmus tests for political acceptability and community acquiesence.

### Relationships between Local Education Authorities and the Department of Education and Science

Another set of trends which merit attention are those in the shifting partnership between the Department of Education and Science and the local education authorities. Relationships between the two seem to be based partially on mutual needs and partially on mutual mistrust. There is some tendency for the relationship based on need to result in greater freedom of action for the local education authority in making decisions. Mistrust in their relationship tends to bring about a hardening of Department of Education and Science views, particularly on matters of finance or in instances of conflict containing potential political embarrassment. But at times, the way in which they act towards each other can only be described in terms of how they are acting towards each other.

The mutual needs the Department of Education and Science and local education authorities are in preserving and promoting the education system as a viable effective enterprise.

While this is implied in law through complementary duties and responsibilities, the statutes do not define practices for cooperation. Obviously, the defence of education from outside attack or serious internal disruption are mutual needs in which both cooperate. The abortive attempt to preserve separate grant support in 1958 is one example, although the Ministry (as it was then) as a central department had to act quietly within the government and had to leave the local education authorities and allied organizations to lead the public fight. When the Burnham Committee faced a deadlock on salaries in 1963 and when the cost of paying teachers frightened local officials, the Minister intervened with greater financial aid and took a seat on the Committee for the Department of Education and Science—that role of player-referee still continues.

The central government, of course, does not want the politically visible role of actually providing the service. It is the local education authority which is the political lightning rod in the implementation of national policies. On a mutual need basis, in exchange for bearing the brunt of controversy, the local education authority is left mainly to its own devices in terms of process. The Department of Education and Science checks which results are achieved, and the next steps in national policy development are influenced by what happens in local authorities. This was the case with secondary reorganization when persuasion was the order of the day through Circular 10/65. Adjustment came in Circular 10/66, adding not only an element of compulsion for recalcitrant authorities but also giving more willing authorities an added weapon with which to influence community opinion (Lewin, 1968, pp. 156-7). Similarly, national and local pressure for nursery education resulted in the withdrawal of the stop order of Circular 8/60. Local authorities were not conforming and, indeed, some were shifting resources into nursery education under several guises.

There is pressure from the Department of Education and Science towards uniformity and national standards, but the rigidity of control prevalent in the 1940s and 1950s has given way to cooperation. In the areas of child or enrolment control, supply and conditions of service for teachers, including quotas, school buildings and school organization, there have been increasing degrees of freedom for local authorities. For example, exceeding the teacher quota in secondary schools used to be considered a 'fiddle' but is now tolerated as long as flagrant abuse is avoided (Brand, 1965, pp. 154-60). Local service requirements vary widely with the size and nature of school population. The Department of Education and Science realizes that central government policies will therefore have a differential impact. Raising the school-leaving age is one example. Some authorities experienced almost no change in numbers of pupils staying on, while others had to absorb many more. The nature of the community, urban or rural, has implications for the types of welfare and ancillary services needed. The necessary freedom of the local education authority to choose how it will provide is recognized by the Department of Education and Science, and even available controls do not seem to be used to limit variations (Boaden, 1970, pp. 184-5).

There is also some expectation that local authorities will be enterprizing in providing services. Specific legislation, narrowly enforced, compels authorities to be more than cautious and to shy away from services they feel desirable and necessary. If there is a promotional aspect in the Department of Education and Science approach, as indicated by Griffith (1966, p. 522), then it should be reflected locally. If Her Majesty's Inspectors through persuasive leadership, consultation and guidance reinforce this aspect in working with schools, as noted by Hartley (1972, p. 450), then the range of choices open to local officials is expanded. The results of this approach seems to be readily observed in a number of activities at the local level including varieties of sixth-form provision, reform of local inspectorates, development of mode III courses, improved in-service training for teachers and introduction of middle school organization.

The obverse need of local authorities is money and the use of DES power to endorse what is being done. Financial needs always seem to outstrip the available money. The rate support grant system, operated through the Department of the Environment, and financing mechanisms available to the Department of Education and Science limit its ability to put funds behind desires for obtaining national objectives. Moreover, it does not have the means to encourage new ideas with financial support (Birley, 1970, p. 29). If basic financing is adequate, authorities can be induced to move in desired directions or to undertake new departures using a greater share of local monies to support development. The basis for inducement is in the understanding that the Department of Education and Science will consult and will stand behind local decisions when and if criticism is levelled at either the expenditure or the idea.

These might all be labelled positive aspects of central-local relationships. In strict terms, it might be said that they result because negative sanctions available to the Department of Education and Science are not applied '. . . but everyone knows where the whip hand lies—and acts accordingly' (Robson, 1968, p. 56). However, it seems preferable to say that, based on mutual recognition of mutual needs, these cooperative aspects have begun to take on the patina of conventions.

Mutual mistrust in relationships between the two arises out of the fact that the Department of Education and Science as a central department does what the government of the day wants done. As ministers follow their interests, the local authorities are brought into line and 'the relationship is determined by what departments decide are their necessary functions' (Griffith, 1966, pp. 506-7). Where interests diverge, conflict can set in. Where conflict goes unresolved and sanctions are applied, the Department of Education and Science may be accused of bad faith in consultations and interference in local administrative matters. This was the response of West Ham when its proposals for new facilities were cut (Peschek and Brand, 1966, p. 68). In fact, the hardness of the Department of Education and Science in the area of major building programme approval is a source of mistrust by local officials. Priorities set by the Secretary of State and granting of permission to borrow by the Department of the Environment seem to be dictated more by the government's assessment of national economic conditions than by any rationale of educational needs. The hardships brought on authorities by these decisions often forces them to crib by using minor works' money to keep roofs over heads.

The Department of Education and Science mistrusts local authorities because their political processes are unpredictable. Even after careful consultation, a council can still respond with outright defiance or half-way measures. At the same time, local officials can make the Department assume the role of ogre by telling the people that the central government is telling the council how to spend the rate-payers' money. This is considered bad form, but it is quite impossible for the Department to tell its side of the story in the community. If forced to bring the local education authority into line, the Department knows that the tools available to it are clumsy, i.e. withholding approvals, filing reports, going to the courts, which in themselves can be used as examples of insensitivity to local needs. In the long term, the central government has the power to bring the authority into line, but in doing so it has to calculate the political costs to its relationships with all authorities.

Both mutual need and mutual mistrust in the relationships between the Department of Education and Science and local authorities provide the local education authorities with a role in policy-making which exceeds legal prescriptions. The central-local partnership viewed in this way implies a local autonomy in which community factors such as perceived needs, degree of political control and council committee structure and procedures can greatly influence policy-making for education, and it leaves a large arena where party political control becomes important (Boaden, 1970, pp. 184-5; 1971, p. 47). If a national consensus about education is weak or lacking, a local education authority may successfully exploit the possibilities of departing from Department of Education and Science policies if it is consistent in its political purposes, if it uses a high level of administrative expertise in stating its problems and if it is willing to use some of its own resources (Wood, 1973, p. 115). Such exploitation through local policy processes can go far in shaping education at the operating end of the system.

### Local Government in Change

Trends in the structure and operation of local government itself are changing the context in which the policy process for education takes place. A new importance is beginning to be attached to the local authority both as a unit of government and as a political entity. The start of this change was the reorganization of 1974. Three reports, an Act of Parliament and a shadow election were the most visible signs that a quarter-century of talk about reform had finally resulted in action.

The *Report* of the Royal Commission on Local Government in England (1969) (Cmnd. 4040) was published in 1969. The Commission, chaired by Lord Redcliffe-Maud, after some three years' work, supplied the basic concepts for reorganization. The report and related research recommended 58 unitary areas and 20 metropolitan districts based on towns and population concentrations. The purpose was to bring the government into line with modern conditions by placing relatively similar-sized populations, sufficiently large to warrant the full range of personal and environmental services, under one authority. In particular, there was some hope that the 'soft' areas of governmental responsibility—education, health, housing and social services—would be lodged at one level of local control for maximum coordination. A lessening of central control was also envisaged as the new authorities would be capable of effectively carrying out broader policy and administrative responsibilities. While radical boundary changes to achieve unitary governments were unacceptable to local government associations, particularly the County Councils Association, the rationalization of services was endorsed (Brand, 1974, pp. 123-8).

The question of improving the operation of local government was also taken up in this period of reform. The Committee on the Management of Local Government, chaired by the then Sir John Maud, had sought earlier to streamline the committee system of local councils and their management. The report in 1967 dealt with modifications in the existing authorities. The key concept was the recommended establishment of a management board of five to nine council leaders to formulate objectives, to coordinate the several committees and to review the progress of the authority towards its objectives. There was to be a chief executive officer to supervise the effectiveness of the paid service in achieving the objectives through what became known as a corporate management approach (The Committee on the Management of Local Government, 1967a, pp. 42-4). However, the design was not widely accepted as it seemed to reduce severely the roles of other committees and of individual members.

As reorganization moved towards legislation, the Study Group on Local Authority Management Structures was set up. Popularly known as the Bains Committee, its task was to advise the new authorities on management structures, while presenting alternatives to the Maud Committee recommendations. Basically, its report *The New Local Authorities: Management and Structure* (The Study Group on Local Authority Management Structures, 1972) held to the original concepts of streamlining, but its proposed policy and resources committee was more closely related to the service committees. The Bains concept of reducing separatism in the committee system, while retaining policy development in the service committees, placed emphasis on councillors' roles and interaction with officers in a corporate structure. The key was not in control but rather in the provision of a number of settings in which members play these roles and carry out tasks. The policy and resources committee of Bains, with the same general functions as the management board of Maud, was thus made more palatable by removing the connotation that it was to be solely a leadership group.

Reorganization was implemented by the Local Government Act of 1972. Instead of a smaller number of unitary authorities, it set up two-level governments of 36 metropolitan districts within 6 metropolitan counties and 39 non-metropolitan counties. Populations varied more than had seemed desirable in the Royal Commission Report, from 1,250,000 to a little over 100,000. The 'soft' areas of governmental responsibility were split up. Housing in the non-metropolitan counties was placed at the district level, while its planning and coordination stayed with the county. A separate Health Services Reorganization Act put health services outside the concern of local government. Only education and social services remained together at the metropolitan district level and at the non-metropolitan county level.

Results for education were mixed. The total number of local education authorities was reduced from 164 to 104—the 39 non-metropolitan counties, the 36 metropolitan districts plus the 20 Outer London boroughs and the Inner London Education Authority which had been created in 1965 and 8 reorganized Welsh counties. Their size variations and the smallness of some (under 250,000 population for nearly all London boroughs and about 50 others under 500,000) did not seem to provide the resource bases which would strengthen them in relation to central government. The education committee was preserved as a statutory committee and the chief education officer as a mandatory appointment. This had been a hard struggle for educators as both Maud and Bains recommended elimination of the compulsory elements. (However, the Association of Education Committees which led the fight, was elbowed out of further implementation consultations by the Association of Municipal Corporations and others.) Local authorities had already begun to experiment with new management structures. The imponderable concern was the relatively unknown and untried relationships between education and the policy committee. To some in sympathy with separateness for education within local government, the Maud doctrine and, to a lesser extent, the Bains doctrine represented potentials for the subjugation of education to non-educational interests. At worst, those interests could be narrowly party political and, at least, could mean the encroachment of management technicians on the professional aspects of operating the education service.

Turning to politics, throughout the several years of study and discussion of reorganization prior to the passage of the Act, political changes were kept in the background. The three parties were more or less planning strategies to improve their holdings in localities. Labour, always strong in its interest in local government, hoped to do better than it did in the London boroughs following the reorganization of 1965. The Conservatives wanted to remain in power in the counties or at least to make sure that their Independent friends did. The reviving Liberals with their notion of community politics felt that they might find more renewal through some gains at the local level. These aspirations were muted because, although all were committed to reorganization, the decisions about reorganizing and the timing of the change-over were political decisions to be made by the party which controlled the government of the day.

Going into the general election of 1970, the Labour government was mainly ready to follow the Redcliffe–Maud proposals, but the Conservatives won control of Parliament. The February 1971 White Paper on reorganization (Cmnd. 4584), issued by the new government, gave little indication of what the Act would look like. In political terms, the Conservatives, in a style reminiscent of an American gerrymander, redrew the lines, apparently basing reorganization on giving the large conurbations over to Labour (which controlled most of them anyway) and of reserving the countryside to themselves. This meant that education and social services, to be governed at the county level outside the metropolitan areas, would be under Conservative control (*Sunday Times*, 31 March 1974). When the bill was put through, the run-up to 'R' day, 1 April 1974, began and with it the struggle for political control of the new authorities.

Without a doubt the shadow elections of 1973 in England and Wales were a dramatic leap in party political control at the local

## Table 1
### Party political control of county councils, England and Wales; 1967, 1970, 1973

| | 1967 | 1970 | 1973 | | |
| | England and Wales | England and Wales | England | | Welsh Counties |
| | | | Metropolitan counties | Non-metropolitan counties | |
| | (58) | (58) | (6) | (39) | (8) |
|---|---|---|---|---|---|
| Labour | 3 | 3 | 6[a] | 7 | 4 |
| Conservative | 14 | 16 | | 18 | |
| Independent (including local party) | 22 | 18 | | 3 | 1 |
| Conservative and Independent | 8 | 5 | | 6 | |
| Multi-party | 2 | 3 | | 3 | 1 |
| Not known, not reported | 9 | 13 | | 2 | 2 |

[a] Of the 36 metropolitan districts which make up these counties, 26 are controlled by Labour, 6 by the Conservatives, 1 by the Liberals and in the remaining 3 no dominant party emerged from the election.

Sources: The Labour Party, the Conservative Party and *The Municipal Yearbook* for appropriate years.

## Table 2
### Candidates for contested seats, county council elections, 1967, 1970; non-metropolitan counties, metropolitan districts, 1973; England and Wales

| | 1967 | 1970 | 1973 | | | |
| | England and Wales | England and Wales | England | | | Welsh Counties |
| | | | Non-metropolitan counties | Metropolitan counties | Metropolitan districts | |
| Seats | 3818 | 3819 | 3129 | 601 | 2517 | 578 |
|---|---|---|---|---|---|---|
| Labour (unopposed) | 1773 (406) | 1500 (216) | 2493 (112) | 596 (20) | 2452 (137) | 445 (94) |
| Conservative[a] (unopposed)[a] | 1322 (676) | 1314 (901) | 3016 (228) | 549 (2) | | 139 (9) |
| Independent (unopposed) | 713 (806) | 729 (800) | 715 (58) | 35 (0) | | 423 (36) |
| Liberal (unopposed) | 288 (27) | 235 (35) | 854 (3) | 200 (0) | | 58 (1) |
| Other (unopposed) | 63 (2) | 107 (4) | 192 (1) | 137 (0) | | 145 (1) |

[a] Includes Independents with Conservative support.

Sources: The Conservative Party, the Labour Party.

level. The contested seats for the new county councils rose to 87.8%, 12.9% more than for the last local elections. Moreover, the number of Independent candidates standing unopposed dropped from 800 to 94. Labour made gains in the countryside, as experienced borough councillors sought county council seats. The elimination of the aldermanic bench, provided in the Act, reduced Conservative strength more than it reduced Labour strength. Labour, which held 3 counties in 1967, won 11 counties including all 6 new metropolitan counties. Within those, Labour won 26 metropolitan districts and the Conservatives 6. The Conservatives won majority control in 18 counties and in 6 others held control with Independent support. Independents, including local parties, who controlled 22 counties in 1967 were reduced to holding 4 counties.

The Maud Committee studies indicated that 'party politics extend to lower levels of decision-taking in local authorities in England and Wales than they do in the other countries . . . examined' (The Committee on the Management of Local Government, 1967a, p. 106). This fact was reinforced in 1973 election contests. Also borne out was the contention that reorganization into fewer but larger local authorities would raise the proportion of authorities run on party political lines (The Committee on the Management of Local Government, 1967b, p. 111). This trend does not necessarily mean that local organizations and operations mimic national parties. They may adhere to party philosophy and may use the advisory services of party headquarters, but, as Birch (1959, p. 44) noted, the major parties are at the local level self-contained, they are busy with their own affairs and they are 'not greatly troubled from day to day by party leaders, party bureaucracy or even by party policy'. Bulpitt (1967, p. 95) came to a similar conclusion, stressing local party individuality and the fact that parties responded more to their environment than to central office directives.

More doctrinaire approaches may be coming. The first task of any party is to win elections and to keep winning them. Clear identification of a party with its philosophy and purposes is a prerequisite in facing the electors. The elections in 1973 indicate that local authorities have become more important as political entities, and what happens in them is politically important. Restraint in partisanship, a tradition in local government, can easily disappear when the stakes are large and when there are advantages to be gained. In the new larger authorities with broader policy responsibilities, this may mean that the contesting parties will display more partisan approaches to enhance their identification. Local conditions will continue to temper party actions but 'no one should be surprised to witness a growing pervasiveness of party spirit' (Heclo, 1969, p. 194). The full implications of party politics and how these will affect the decision process for education is still unfolding (Jennings, 1975, pp. 33–7).

## Summary

The question of politics and the policy process in local education authorities has been raised. The limited understanding of the process by which decisions are made has become increasingly critical as interest in the role of education in the society multiplies. In part, the lack of understanding has arisen because the prescriptions for the governance of education are less than useful descriptions of its governance. The dynamics of policy-making at the local level require examination in order to begin the development of a more complete picture.

The context in which local decision-making for education takes place has undergone vast change between 1960 and 1975. The national consensus of the 1960s has disappeared, and its disappearance is reflected in more polarized national party stances. Interest in education by the central government has diminished, leaving local government with more of the stresses that accumulate at the operating end of the education system. Relationships between the Department of Education and Science and local education authorities, while moving towards recognition of local needs and cooperation as a basis, have developed mistrust of each others' political processes. The net result is in the direction of greater implied local education authority autonomy. The rush of politics into education questions at the local level has shifted the manner in which those questions are faced. Party politics are a relatively new ingredient in deciding the steps to be taken in making educational policy, and reorganization of local government in 1974 raised party political involvement to new heights. The effects of these changes have begun to emerge, and their impact will be observed in succeeding chapters which examine the mix of politics and policy-making for education at the local level.

Having raised the topic of policy, it seems necessary in chapter 2 to present several views of what policy is and what its functions are in local government. The discussion will be followed with the introduction of a six-stage model of the policy process and a preview of the participants in policy-making.

# 2 Policy and a Process Model

There is relatively broad agreement among students and practitioners of government on what the word policy means, lending at least conceptual clarity to what the end product should look like. There is also reasonable agreement about the functions of policy or what the existence policies means in the conduct of local government. However, there is considerable difficulty with the questions of who participates in raising and responding to policy concerns, what the participants contribute to and how they arrive at the decisions necessary in making policy. These are parts of the process, and they are questions which cannot be fully answered by looking at definitions of policy or the formal policy-making structure.

Much of the study and discussion of local government re-organization has centred on ways of improving policy-making structures. The emphasis on policy committees, on corporate management and on the roles of elected members and officers has brought policy into renewed prominence as a matter which local authorities should develop and use for bettering their performance. The pragmatic task of setting policy through these changed structures is still being tried and tested. Yet, the Maud report, by exposing the myth in the traditional distinction between policy-makers and policy administrators (The Committee on the Management of Local Government, 1967a, p. 38), opened the way for reconsideration of the process through its functional and operational aspects from initiation to implementation. The formal decision-makers in government remain most significant in the process, but the roles they carry out can now be seen as differing from those expected under the old dichotomy of politician and officer.

It is through these larger functional and operational aspects that questions about the process and the participants' roles can be answered. Stating what policy is and what its functions are in local government yields some initial clues to the various process decisions necessary. By modelling the policy process, the potential of the varied roles of policy-makers in government and with the public begins to emerge. An examination of selected literature about the participants in the process provides a basis for later discussion of their interrelationships in taking decisions.


## Policy

Policy is a guide for taking future actions and for making appropriate choices or decisions towards the accomplishment of some intended or desired end. Policy may also be thought of as setting out solutions to a problem, i.e. it is the intent of policy-makers to change existing conditions in ways which will solve a problem. Policies are normative in that they are statements of what should or ought to be; thus they imply value bases. However, policies are not decisions for single separate actions, nor are they goals in the larger sense. Policy has three characteristics which distinguish it from goals on the one hand and separate detailed decisions on the other. First, policy has an aspect of giving direction to choosing or deciding. Goals, value positions or philosophically stated ends, from which policy is usually derived, by themselves provide no direction for their achievement. Stating a policy or policies has the effect of indicating the choices that are preferrable in terms of what is to be achieved (Heclo, 1972, p. 84). Policy itself is not a course of action, but action results as choices or decisions are made, tested and put into operation. Second, policy has a future orientation. Notions of intent and of accomplishment over time or at some later time mean that a series of choices or decisions are expected and required. Policy is made in anticipation of the necessity for making sets of decisions articulated one with another in the development of appropriate courses of action. Third, policy allows for changes in the context of decision-making. This property is not found in the absoluteness of goals, while separate detailed decisions are often direct responses to particular factors. Policy as a guide implies that the context, the changing socioeconomic and political setting, will be reviewed from time to time as the results of previous choices or decisions are observed and as further choices or decisions are needed.

Policy as problem-solving can be said to set out certain conditions to be changed or needs to be fulfilled. The extent to which the authority determines that it will meet those needs and the resources that it will allocate to do this are the ingredients of policy. From such a policy flows the decisions and from the decisions the actions (Stewart, 1972, p. vi). If the policy indicates, as it may, the kinds of activities required, it seems an easy step to identify the combinations of services and to perform them; thus policy may also provide a focus for coordination of services. Policy as solutions to problems requires a great deal of specificity in its making, and constraints on information as well as uncertainty in projections of future resource needs can prove difficult. A fair degree of accuracy is a prerequisite, because the guides to action are more in the nature of controls designed to produce detailed decisions.

There are also gradations or levels of policy that are spoken of in common usage. General or basic policy is overarching and indicates a great degree of goal-relatedness. It has broad applicability to the entire organization and little in the way of specification as to actions. In addition, there is administrative policy which is thought to be more detailed as to what is to be done, where and by whom. The two levels are not mutually exclusive in definition or application, and in many instances it is difficult to find a clear line of demarcation between them. The most usual division that local officials seem to make is between authority-wide policy, pertaining to an intended objective and applicable in all services or departments, and administrative policy that controls or regulates the manner in which departments or services will operate in respect of carrying out any number of authority policies. A policy on land use to ensure sufficient recreation areas would be an authority-wide policy; whereas a personnel policy might be considered an administrative policy, to regulate staff hiring procedures. Then, too, a department such as housing might have administrative policies dealing with land use which would detail how that department is to operate within authority-wide policy, e.g. provision of an open space for recreation in council housing projects and regulation of the hours of operation for recreation grounds. The situation is similar in standing orders. They tend to be administrative policies for the conduct of authority business but often contain or imply general policies indicating authority intent or objectives.

The rationale for devising administrative policy is to provide further direction at the operational level. There is some expectation that administrative policy will be derived from basic or general policy. Once an intent or purpose has been chosen, there is the necessity of establishing controls over various activities to ensure, in so far as possible, that those activities are directed towards the ends designated by the policy. In general, administrative policy is a control on action, so that the administrator can distinguish when and how to act from when and where to look for further policy guidance. The opportunity to test and evaluate decisions and to examine them for their contributions to the achievement of general policy is also provided through administrative policy. This indicates that adminstrative policy may be revised or modified from time to time, while the basic policy remains quite constant. If, when decisions taken have been evaluated or when changes in the background arise, it appears that new combinations of activities are needed, administrative policy can be changed to assure continued control and progress.

There are two further points to be made about policy, both broad general policies and adminstrative policies. First, policies are not always stated, i.e. they are not written down and are not clearly identifiable in documents as intents or decision guides. By reviewing a series of decisions that have been made in a given area of endeavour it may be possible to deduce a policy: the actions taken imply a policy. Inaction or consistent decisions not to act also imply policy. Thus, the intention or purpose may produce a policy without reference to the results which actually occur, the choices neither considered nor made (Heclo, 1972, p. 85). Sometimes these ways of doing may be found fixed in traditions or conventions, because they have been perpetuated without critical reexamination or testing. Yet, they have the effect and force of policy, as they imply certain intended outcomes (Stewart, 1972, p. v).

Second, many policies tends to be prescriptive and thus subject to interpretation. The lack of specificity in intent or action leaves room for manoeuvre on the part of the policy-makers. Often it is the perspectives of the participants and the consistency of their actions that makes policies effective. The testing or review of progress becomes more a matter of judgement than of hard factual evaluation, unless the consequent administrative policies are designed to include evaluative criteria. However, this can only be done if the policy-makers are questioned and pressed to become more specific about the ends to be achieved.

Policy-making, the setting out of intentions and the guides for future actions, is a task of local government and occupies a central position in the actions local authorities take as they provide for services. There is reasonable agreement about the functions of policy and what having policies means in the conduct of local government.

## Policy in Local Government

Policy and the process by which it is made fulfils several functions in the conduct of local government. Every local authority is a provider of services and has the task of deciding how it will support and coordinate those services. Moreover, the authority has the responsibility for designating the larger purposes to which those services will be directed in terms of community needs and well-being. In doing so, the authority may have to recognize national policy or to meet central government minimums for some aspects of some services, but it sets the priorities for what is to be provided and controls the flow of resources to the services (Sharpe, 1973, pp. 166-8). 'The timing, scope, funding and distribution of local government services is . . . far more within the scope of their powers than is commonly recognized in the literature . . .' (Boaden and Alford, 1969, p. 204). The choices made in regard to these factors constitute policies, and these policies together are the range and scope of government.

Policy is not neutral, nor is it made value-free. Since it indicates intent, there must be some bases for choosing one intention from among several alternatives. Community values and norms provide those bases and are part of the situation or the context in which policy is decided (Vickers, 1974, p. 9). Peoples' aspirations as well as their needs, problems and discontents figure in the policy choices made by the government. The policy process functions as a focal point for the sorting out of many of these factors at the community level. It must be remembered, however, that the government has a monopoly on local service provision (Sharpe, 1973, p. 160); thus it controls value allocations and policy choices. While competition among alternatives is not eliminated, it can be limited.

The policies of an authority clarify the direction of community change and development by indicating what is to be done. As needs are identified and peoples' discontents become known, policy is made by the government to bring services into line with community desires. The match with desires may not be perfect, but the expected course of action will tend to be towards these generally acceptable ends rather than towards the opposite. Once the choices are made through the policy process, the activities of government are modified to reflect those choices. Funds are made available, and departments take up new tasks or redirect existing ones to new ends. Services are provided in accordance with specified needs rather than by some random or traditional concept of what should be done.

Policy also sets priorities on what the government will do and which objectives will receive greater or earlier attention compared with other government projects. The sequences in which various projects are to be undertaken and the necessity of attaining a certain standard of provision in an area of endeavour before starting improvements in a related area are often designated through policy choices. Policies can make distinctions between older continuing programmes and new developing programmes that will usually require greater initial resource support. The many activities of an authority are always in competition for its scarce resources. The time, money and talent available to an authority are limited, and so decisions must be made about their allocation. The authority, through the policy process, establishes the needs it intends to fulfil and also the level of achievement. This, in turn, can be translated into the types and amounts of resources required. Policy can assure their appropriate distribution. Reviewing policies and their resource requirements can also forecast the need for obtaining additional resources through recruiting specialized personnel or by increasing the rates.

The statutory obligations of an authority are best carried out under locally made policies. Central government departments often have regulations that require the authority to meet certain conditions or to specify how it will provide for selected aspects of a service. Local policy sets out the specific features to ensure that the regulations are met in a fashion which takes local conditions into account. Where a minimum standard for provision is made mandatory by the central government, local policy clarifies that minimum by defining it within the local situation. On the other hand, when the authority has chosen to exceed the minimum, the existence of a policy safeguards against *de facto* acceptance of the minimum as the objective of the authority. Development of local policy to meet statutory obligations also ensures that the appropriate resources will be allocated to them but within the priorities scheme for supporting all authority activities.

Authority policies provide benchmarks against which to judge governmental performance and progress. These judgements are made not only by local officials but also by the electors. Officers and elected members should be capable of making detailed evaluations and distinctions between appropriate and inappropriate progress. The electors' judgements would be much less refined, because they would be based on generalized understandings of what the authority is trying to accomplish and on rather ill-defined criteria for evaluation. Obviously, when the reports of committees are received, the government compares the results of various programmes and activities with the intent and level of accomplishment implied or stated in the policy. It can then proceed to remedy the situation by revising the policy, by correcting the problems in implementation, by modifying activities and support levels and possibly by changing personnel. The electors may not be so discriminating, as their own frames of reference are connected with what they consider the intent of the authority. Where results achieved through council policies do not measure up to the expectations of the electors, their response or means of remedying the situation is usually limited to changing personnel—through the ballot box. Of course, members of the public can attempt to effect policy change through lobbying by interest groups, by voicing opinions at public hearings and by seeing their council members. Seeking a policy change implies dissatisfaction either with results or with existing policy. The public evaluates council policies mainly on the basis of their contacts with the government and particularly on their feelings about how they have been affected by public services: whether they have received the services they want, whether the quality of those services is what they expect and how much the cost of those services is in terms of their perceived impact on the rates.

At the administrative level, policies are made for regulation of the department activities pursuant to the adoption of a general or basic policy for the authority. These lower-level policies help to identify the kinds of decisions to be made in departments and, to some extent, the routines for handling their responsibilities under the policy. Such policies can go far to ensure consistency of action in similar situations by reducing the judgement factors. When new situations arise that call for different decisions, they can be more readily recognized. If further policy guidance is heeded, the differences between situations can be stated more clearly, so that appropriate solutions can be devised.

Policy at the administrative level also helps to ensure similarity of provision and treatment in cases of similar need. In other words, it it helps to keep priorities in order and services evenly distributed. It also regulates the flow of resources. Cases are examined on their merits, because that is what determines whether or not each case is subject to the existing policy. If a series of cases begin to appear as exceptions to the policy, it may indicate that the policy is not working as expected because conditions have changed. This is a form of evaluation which should bring about some questions, leading to policy modification.

There is another point to providing similar treatment in cases of similar need. The public often judges council services in terms of comparisons between sections of the community or neighbourhoods. If one is perceived as receiving more or less than another in similar circumstances, the council may be accused of favouritism or of not being able to see the parallels in the two situations. The same type of judgement is rendered when some people feel they have been mistreated by officers, case workers, teachers or clerks in the course of obtaining and receiving public services. Again these are evaluations which members of the public make and act upon when the opportunity presents itself—particularly at election time.

Evaluation of services by officials should be provided through administrative policy. The effectiveness of a service in its activities under authority policies should be determined periodically. Criteria for such evaluations are derived from policy and the particular tasks of the department in implementation of that policy. Where such systems as programme budgeting and management by objective are part of the regular administrative control and monitoring procedures, the criteria are included as part of the system. Under other procedures the criteria may have to be generated separately and the evaluative process specified as part of administrative policy. If more than one department is responsible for an activity or where coordination of activities is required, evaluation may be jointly planned. The results of evaluation are used by policy-makers to correct deficiencies in services and/or to modify policies as to their intent. From this point of view, technical information about performance is measured against desired outcomes. Judgements are then made about the possibility of changes in the allocation of resources and the political viability of such changes.

The policies of local government give direction and priority to aspects of community development. Provision of services, allocation of resources to those services and determination of their effectiveness in meeting the requirements of the community are functions which a policy performs. The policies and the directions that will be chosen by the policy-makers out of the many available are determined through the policy-making process.

## A Policy Process Model

There are many decisions which have to be taken in making a policy, decisions that concern how policy will be developed, who will participate in its development and what contributions the participants will make. These decisions are critical in so far as there are many values, attitudes and opinions about what the government should do, which services it should provide and at which levels or standards. Policy-makers in local authorities make the decisions in a process which is essentially political and which has as its purpose to produce 'from a confusion of conflicting and competing views a stream of policy sufficiently coherent to realize one of all the possible combinations of achievement . . .' (Vickers, 1974, p. 6). There are process questions that involve the needs and demands for services in different sections of the community and the standards of service that should be expected. Policy-makers have to sort out the disposition of the authority towards provision of these and to do so they must resolve what are often intragovernment conflicts (Boaden, 1971, pp. 23-5).

The policy-making process can be modelled as a series of steps or stages to illustrate the several different kinds of decisions which have to be made by policy-makers. The model presented here has been adapted from two sources on policy-making in government, Agger *et al.* (1964, pp. 40-51) and Milstein and Jennings (1973, pp. 8-10). It consists of six overlapping stages from initiation to implementation. Each stage raises process questions to which policy-makers respond and, in responding, shape not only outcome of that stage but also influence what happens in succeeding stages.

The first stage, *initiation* of the process, occurs when dissatisfaction is expressed with the present situation. The present policy may be felt to be working an inequity on some segment of the public or may not be adequately fufilling a need. A lack of policy may have the same effect in that a service is not being provided. There may be some expectations for performance, some standard that members of the public or people within the government believe is not being met. The deviation of performance from what is expected may be called a problem. Obviously there are numerous potential sources for voicing dissatisfactions, and the policy-makers have to decide who to listen to and when.

Stage two, *reformulation of opinion*, is when opinions are gathered and begin to crystallize around particular points. The dissatisfactions become more fully articulated as individuals and organizations consolidate their views. Leaders emerge to get something done about the problem. These leaders may be members of the public or local government officials, policy-makers themselves. Some opinion-gathering and opinion-making may be begun by the policy-makers in order to clarify the possible alternative solutions which might be available to them. The range is influenced by limitations in law, availability of resources and political feasibility of acceptance. The policy-makers' initial response may be tested at this point both within the government and outside the government. The decisions to begin opinion-making or to test an initial response carry the risk of preempting certain choices and of denying alternatives, some of which may be proposed by those people who are dissatisfied.

*Emergence of alternatives,* stage three, is when potential solutions to the problem or ways of fulfilling the need are put forward. The dissatisfactions have, by now, been translated into descriptions and statements of what would be acceptable changes and into ways that will alleviate the inequity or will bring performance into line with expectation. Several alternatives may be proposed by those who are dissatisfied. The policy-makers also present alternatives and delineate the one or more choices available. Which proposals they present are, of course, reflective of some assessment of political acceptability both in and out of government. The decisions the policy-makers face at this stage are whether to press on with their alternatives or whether to prepare to consider other alternatives. This decision is made in the light of some assessment of the influence wielded by those who are dissatisfied and the degree of control which the policy-makers feel they can exert over the process through the next two stages.

At the next stage, *discussion and debate,* alternatives are shaped into policy proposals. There may be some combination of alternatives by those leaders who seeking a change of policy. This is done in order to gather increased support or to make the proposals more acceptable to the policy-makers who will make the final considerations. Interested organizations and individuals are mobilized to influence those who will decide. Where proposals are at variance with those of the policy-makers, conflict may set in and may continue until the final choice is made. On the other hand, compromises may be made through consultation or by separate decisions inside and outside the government. Through this stage the policy-makers' proposals become fully developed. Assessments of the situation continue, limits are placed on compromise and modification and the preferred policy proposals are chosen. Consent-building both inside and outside the government begins. The critical decisions for the policy-makers revolve around the limits to be set and the consent-building thought to be necessary.

*Legitimization,* the fifth stage, is the legislation of a policy from among the competing proposals. Selection of the one or more policy proposals for final consideration is made by the policy-makers, and it is the policy-makers who decide what will become the policy. These decisions may be taken by a few influential people in the government or by a group of policy-makers that has power to direct others formally or informally. This choice of policy is then ratified or legislated by a majority of those policy-makers empowered to do so by law. Failure of ratification usually means a return to stage three or four and reassessments of the situation.

*Implementation* of the policy is the sixth and final stage. Whether the policy is announced publicly or not (some policies are merely promulgated within the government), administrative procedures and, perhaps, administrative policies are devised and put into effect by one or more departments of the government.

The process is not static but cyclical. When the policy is ratified and put into effect, it may soon call forth new dissatisfactions or problems. Poor administration, changing circumstances and erosion of confidence in the policy because intended outcomes fail to materialize can lead to renewed demands for another policy change. The process starts again as rival claims and viewpoints are expressed.

The decisions within the process are critical for the policy outcomes and the shaping of governmental services at the operating level. That shaping also reflects political outcomes of the process. As has been noted, the process decisions determine who will participate, what they will contribute and when. Who influences, controls or attempts to control these decision situations therefore becomes critical. In examining the process within English local authorities, it is those policy-makers who command the government machinery that are most likely to control the process. How well they fare, however, depends on their capability to manipulate or use the machinery; committees, departments, expertise, advice, consultation, conventions, debate, etc., not so much in a technical sense but in a political sense.

It is from the perspective of the political manipulation and control of the policy process in local government that policy-making for education is being examined. How central participants, elected members and officers, carry out the various interrelated roles and activities is a key to understanding the process. As will be seen, how they deal with each other is, in many ways, more critical than how they deal with the public and those agencies and organizations outside the local government.

## The Policy-Makers

The participants in the policy process for education at the local level are many. Their potential contributions and the decisions they might make at each stage of the process arise out of a variety of roles and activities in which they are engaged. The policy-makers, citizens, elected members, officers, and their various roles are introduced here. Their activities, the interactions and the influences they exert and the kinds of decisions they help to make will be detailed later.

Members of the public have several roles, each with its own potential impact on the policy process. Their most generalized role and the one with decisive impact is that of the elector. The electors are the final arbiters of policy when they vote every four years. Through the ballot box they determine whether the directions of local policy-making will continue as it has under the incumbents or whether a new direction will be sought under a new set of office-holders. There is evidence that local elections tend⁷ to follow national swings in political sentiments, and councillors also believe that electors vote by party label or on some assessment of national politics (Dearlove, 1973, p. 42). Yet, councillors believe that local party stands on local matters are examined by the electors and this forms a basis for the way they vote. In councillors' views, their representational roles as well as their constituent case work are important factors in electors' judgements (Cole, 1956, p. 174; Heclo, 1969, p. 197). Certainly, when it comes to the question of setting the rates, controlling parties have been known to turn away from actions which would raise them 'for fear of losing votes' (Peschek and Brand, 1966, p. 90). Thus, while the electors may vote on many different bases, the result is an elected body which tends to act as the representation of the constituents' interests (Sharpe, 1973, p. 170). The electors are not ignored when policy is being made.

The interest of the general public in education issues does not seem to be consistently high, and its knowledge of the education service is low (Boaden, 1971, p. 48). When issues arise, elected representatives seem to act as a shield to protect education from direct social pressure (Eggleston in Baron and Taylor, 1969, p. 19). Mobilization of public opinion is a purpose of interest groups, and, when members of the public are organized as interest groups, there is some evidence that they can influence the actions of local officials. Blatant pressure such as mass protests are not appreciated and are not listened to by councils (Peterson and Kantor, 1970, p. 13), and a campaign through the news media or the threat of court suits seems to produce little effect (Lewin, 1968, p. 147). However, where the interest groups have limited objectives, e.g. to be consulted on aspects of education rather than to seek wholesale modification of proposals, they seem to have greater opportunity for influencing the outcomes. The subtle pressure of parents' organizations seems to operate in this fashion (Saran, 1967, p. 402). While local coalitions are rare, actions of interest groups, combined with other factors, can bring pressure to bear. If there is assistance from national affiliates, the influence on community opinion can be considerable (Eggleston, 1966, p. 946). If access to the government seems difficult to obtain, officers provide one route (Peschek and Brand, 1966, p. 95), but other routes seem to open or close as local officials decide (Dearlove, 1973, p. 201). Consultation, then, may become the 'pill-sweetener' dispensed to interest groups by the politicians (Batley et al., 1970, p. 98).

Perhaps the most heralded participation by members of the public is through cooptation onto the education committee. The places reserved for persons who are interested and knowledgeable in education are filled by committee and the council appointment. Local education authorities have shown little enthusiasm for cooptation, and the persons appointed are often selected for their past service and sympathy with the majority party. Coopted members' votes rarely stray from majority wishes (Peterson and Kantor, 1970, pp. 10–11). The contributions of coopted members as channels for community opinion and as presenters of alternatives are not convincing. However, they may have some moderating influence on the doctrinaire excesses of parties.

Elected members of local councils fill many different roles, all of which have some bearing on their policy-making activities. Among the roles that they play are as representatives for the constituents of their wards, as members of their party groups and as committee members who decide about a service and who follow their interests in a particular aspect of governmental endeavour. Some members take a leadership role such as a committee chairman, a shadow chairman or a spokesman if a member of the minority, a party leader in the council, a member of the policy and resources committee, a member of the executive or policy committee of the party group. The representational role, serving a geographical area or social segment of the community, is a generalized role. The needs of their area and the dissatisfactions of its people are identified through it. Specialized interests of members are reflected in their committee work and in the particular policies they attempt to promote (Heclo, 1969, p. 188; Jones, 1973, pp. 140-1). In the committee, members are also supposed to review the discretionary functions of officers and to support loyally party views and the party leadership (Self, 1971, p. 277). This is difficult as party views may conflict with officers' advice, with the interests of constituents or even with the member's own special knowledge on a topic. Members selected for leadership roles have dual responsibilities in the committee system of local government and in their party group. Chairmen of committees regulate the agenda and workload of their committees. They also have the important task of keeping their majority members in line behind party programmes throughout the discussion of issues and policies. How influential a committee chairman is and how powerful the committee can become in providing and directing a service depends on the degree of party control exercised by the majority party (Maddick and Pritchard, 1958, p. 150).

This holds true for the education committee, too, in spite of the tradition of autonomy it has as a statutory committee. The chairman's most critical task is in working with the principal officers to obtain advice and opinions for operation of the service. Often, it is the chairman and the chief officer who cooperate in initiating policy alternatives for committee consideration (The Committee on the Management of Local Government, 1967b, p. 196). At times, they may be in conflict when political views do not agree with expert views on need and necessary action (Boaden, 1971, p. 25). Chairmen may find it difficult to keep themselves from administering and from specifying department activities which are traditionally the province of the officers. On the other hand, committee members often fear that chairmen are led to decisions by officers rather than that they are guided by the committee (Birley, 1970, p. 31). Minority spokesman or shadow chairmen have the more limited role of maintaining vigilance on the part of their members where there are party differences on major issues and of judging when to seek amendments to items that they feel might be successfully modified. On routine matters, the minority often agrees to the action proposed by the chairman. One complaint frequently heard is that the relationship between the chairman and the chief officer gives the majority an advantage in having professional advice while in effect denying it to the minority (The Committee on the Management of Local Government, 1967a, p. 113).

Party leaders in the council have the role of keeping their members together and of making effective us of the government machinery to promote stated ends. Majority party leaders often hold the chairmanships of important committees such as policy and resources or finance. From there they seek to exercise a degree of control over key issues or proposals in governmental activity. Majority leaders also exercise influence over other committee chairmanships both in appointments and in regulating the scope of committee matters which come under the heading of policy-making (The Committee on the Management of Local Government, 1967b, pp. 110–11). Budgetary considerations are most often a focus for the application of influence and control. Occasionally, leaders have to step into disputes between committees. Minority leaders often serve on policy and resources or on finance committees where they express their party's views while using the position as a listening post to majority proposals. This information is shared with committee shadow chairmen or spokesmen for their use in guiding minority actions. Both majority and minority leaders are, however, subject to some degree of control by their respective party groups.

Members and their leaders meet together in party groups. While the party groups are outside the government, what occurs in them has a direct bearing on committee deliberations and policy direction in the local authority. Each party in the council decides its stands on issues and defines how it expects its members to act on issues. Often, the committee chairmen or shadow chairmen have the responsibility of keeping their party colleagues informed about developments in the committee's area of endeavour (Wiseman, 1963a, pp. 63–4). The group decides on its stance by examining current proposals in the light of what they believe to be party philosophy, aims and general direction. The party leader, sometimes individually and sometimes as a member of a group executive or policy committee, may present recommended positions for the guidance of party members in council. When approved by the group, adherence to these is expected of each member (The Committee on the Management of Local Government, 1967a, p. 114; 1967b, pp. 103, 607). However, if a doctrinaire approach is taken without other considerations being made, there could be political repercussions in store for the party.

Officers administer the departments of local authorities and manage the actual delivery of services. Chief officers and their top-level assistants are appointed by the council. As professional experts in their fields they are expected to serve the authority, advising elected members in the committee and in the council regardless of party control. This tradition has rarely been broken, although at times it is badly bent by majority party monopoly and manipulation. Officers, particularly the chief education officer, have several roles which bear on policy process decisions. It is as professionals that they identify needs for changes in the service and for resources to operate the service and that they bring those needs to the attention of their committee. The officers also plan for the future provision of services by keeping track of trends and by evaluating present provision. These items are usually put before the committee in regular reports. More importantly, chief officers advise and recommend on policy alternatives either at the request of the committee or out of their own perceptions of possible directions.

Officers have 'concern for the professional values in their work . . . ' and some desire 'to see their sphere of work expand and develop' (Boaden, 1971, p. 32). This concern often appears in recommendations; sometimes it is hedged in order to be politically palatable, sometimes not. Options are spelled out in terms of resource requirements, expected outcomes and activities that might be undertaken. While the questions raised are to be answered by members, especially those questions with a political content, the chief officer's advice can condition or direct the answers (Brand, 1965, pp. 139-40). Thus a situation often exists where the chief officer, as an expert, defines the problem and the alternative solutions and sets out the probable consequences of the alternatives (Heclo, 1969, p. 189), However, advice is not policy. On technical matters, an officer's advice may rarely be questioned, but in reaching policy decisions the committee, the chairman and the interaction with officers are important factors (Maddick and Pritchard, 1958, pp. 149-50; The Committee on the Management of Local Government, 1967b, p. 157).

There is little doubt that chief education officers should be counted as policy-makers. They play a prominent part in the process not only through committee but also through briefing the chairman for presenting education's case in the policy and resources committee or in the council. The chief education officer's assessments cannot help but be taken into account by the party groups and by majority and minority leaders on the committee. Political party control is, however, a check against bureaucracy and professional syndicalism in local government (Cole, 1956, p. 174; Sharpe, 1973, p. 174).

Chief education officers seem to delegate few decision-making activities. The flow of information and opinions, the timing or pacing of their presentation and the suggestions for consultation can usually be controlled by the chief education officer (Lewin, 1968, pp. 170-1). Interpretation of the Department of Education and Science regulations and of teachers' views and parental reactions are also made by the chief education officer. These presentations can be disputed by members, but members do not often have easy access to information sources.

The increase in party political control tends to decrease the necessity for the chief officer to be supersensitive to personal politics and to members' interests, because such political concerns are increasingly being handled in groups where officers are not present (Maddick and Pritchard, 1958, pp. 148, 154). The committee provides similar checks on purely professional solutions, and it reviews performance; with all parties represented, this ensures continuous political control (Jones, 1973, pp. 140, 143). Yet the chief education officer in carrying out his role is still very much involved in activities conditioned by political factors and '. . . resolved by some form of political process' (Baron and Taylor, 1969, p. 7). The committee, together with the chairman, is a significant point of political contact, a link to the party and the party line and a place to test actions and reactions in the political sense (Jones, 1973, pp. 143-4). How the chief education officer fares in the decision-taking that is the policy process may be more dependent on these kinds of links than on professional expertise. The process decisions made or influenced by the chief education officer are critical to his role as a policy-maker.

## Summary

The definition of policy and the descriptions of its functions in local government indicated that the scope and shape of services are regulated by policy decisions. The many competing societal concerns, needs and special interests have to be sorted out through the policy process before objectives and guides for government action—policies—can be stated. A six-stage model of the policy process, from initiation to implementation, was presented as a frame for identifying the kinds of decisions necessary in reaching a policy. It also emphasized that the process has many potential participants, each of whom can have an impact on policy through the decisions which comprise the process. Members of the public, elected members of the council and local government officers were introduced in their various roles as policy-makers.

It was noted that the policy process is a political process. The interrelationships of the participants were focused on by considerations of influence and control. This interaction is focused on local government. In chapter 3 the local authority will be examined as a policy centre from two aspects: policy-making power in education and organization for policy-making. These aspects will be set against the imperatives of party political control at the local level. The perceptions of elected members, officers and others in the six authorities studied will be used together with the literature to explain the interplay of politics and local government organization.

# 3 The Local Authority as a Policy Centre

The local authority, as a policy centre, legislates policies for application in its geographical area. The council has the power to act as a government under the statutes except that it may not act *ultra vires*, i.e. beyond those powers given in the statutes. Organizationally, the authority is structured to make and carry out policy decisions. Through the committee system, elected representatives advised by professional officers recommend policies and activities for the provision of services by the council.

Local authority policy-making takes place in a political framework, and the process of policy-making is a political one. The political parties and their orientations towards social questions and towards local government are basic factors in the framework. Gaining and retaining control of government is the focus of party activity, and the policy process is the vehicle for stamping the party imprint on the activities of government. Thus the way in which parties manage and maintain the extension of political control into the committee structure is critical to understanding the policy process.

In examining the local authority as a policy centre, this chapter initially outlines the council's formal powers in education. The committee structure, the functional committees—finance, establishment, policy and resources—and the education committee-complex as well as the administrative organization, the education department, are then described. Within the structure, the posts and particular committees which link the system together will be identified. Next, political parties in the local government will be discussed, and examination will be made of the mechanisms they have for harnessing the committee system to political decision-making. These aspects will be illustrated with information gathered in the six local authorities, three counties and three Outer London boroughs, during the course of the study. From this material, the political frame of influence, action and maintenance of control will be obtained.

## Powers and Duties in Education

The Education Act of 1902 established the governmental structure for a national system of local education by making the then county and borough councils into the local authorities for elementary and secondary education. These all-purpose local governments, established in 1888, were reorganized in 1974 with the result that the education authorities for England and Wales outside the Greater London area are now the 47 county councils and the 36 metropolitan district councils. The reorganization of Greater London government in 1965 created the Inner London Education Authority and the 20 Outer London boroughs with responsibility for education.

The powers and duties of local education authorities stem from the Education Act of 1944. Although some of its provisions have been conditioned by other acts and have been restricted procedurally by regulations, it remains the basic law for the government of education. The local education authority is empowered as follows.

(1) To control secular education in state schools (with the exception of voluntary-aided secondary schools).
(2) To provide for the management of schools and to group schools for management under one board.
(3) To inspect schools maintained by the authority.
(4) To control the appointment of teachers; to draw up detailed conditions of service for teachers an non-teaching personnel.
(5) To establish new schools, to determine the types of schools to be built, to change the character and purpose of state schools and to cease to maintain a school or schools.
(6) To purchase compulsorily the land necessary for approved educational purposes.
(7) To make special arrangements for the education of children

with special needs and to provide board, lodging and clothing if necessary.

(8) To stop the employment of children which is deemed prejudicial to their obtaining the benefits of education.

(9) To make grants and to pay expenses of children to enable them to participate in local school activities or to attend independent schools.

(10) To conduct or assist in research and to organize educational conferences.

The duties of local education authorities include the following.

(1) To provide full-time primary and secondary schools of appropriate number and type, equipped to give all pupils an education through the varieties of instruction which is made desirable by their different ages, aptitudes and abilities; this extends to providing nursery schools, special schools for the handicapped and boarding school accommodation for pupils considered by their parents and the authority to require it.

(2) To ascertain which children need special education treatment.

(3) To make instruments and articles of government for the management or government of schools.

(4) To provide medical inspection and treatment for pupils.

(5) To offer, where necessary, transportation for pupils or to pay travel expenses of pupils.

(6) To see that parents carry out their duties with regard to the attendance of compulsory school-age children.

(7) To make arrangements for further education; to carry out directions of the Secretary of State requiring provision or to help in maintaining a teachers' training institution.

(8) To make development plans for the area.

(9) To appoint a chief education officer.

(10) To keep accounts of all monies received and spent.

All these powers and duties are areas for policy-making. There are procedures which must be included in some; certain approvals must be obtained from the Secretary of State, but initiation rests with the authority. For example, a change in the character of a school requires publication of a notice to the public and approval by the Department of Education and Science under Section 13 of the Act, but it is the authority which decides to change and which designates the new character of the school.

On the other hand, placing pupils in direct-grant schools at parental request and paying the fees is strictly a matter of local authority determination.

Although these powers and duties are given to local councils by the 1944 Act, the education committee of the council carries out the tasks of developing and recommending policies. As a statutory committee, its reports must be considered by the council before action is taken. The council may authorize the committee to exercise the council's functions in education except for borrowing money or for raising rates. In practice, resource allocations (money, land and personnel) tend to be decided by recommendation of other council committees reviewing the requests of the education committee. Thus, while education controls the establishment of teaching positions, the creation of ancillary posts such as groundsmen or school meals service cooks requested by education must be approved by the establishment committee and must be included in the estimates as approved by the finance or the policy and resources committee. In addition, selection of building sites, although within the power of the education committee, has to be coordinated with the broader planning and development schemes of the authority through the appropriate council committees. Health, welfare, recreation and other social services, especially where they affect children and youth, are further areas for cooperation and coordination with the committees responsible for their provision (Birley, 1970, pp. 26–34). The result is that education while enjoying broad powers operates within the constraints of the local government structure. That structure is examined next.

## The Committee Structure of Local Government

The council is the ultimate policy-deciding body in every local authority. It acts almost exclusively on reports received from its committees, many times without further debate or deliberation. Members may raise questions about a report or some specific point in a recommendation, a faction of the council or the minority party may make a public show of opposition by speeches and the majority leader may respond with praise for the committee's keen grasp of community needs. However, the final outcome is almost always a foregone conclusion: the action that committees recommend as policy is ratified by the council.

It is the committee system of the council that is at the heart of the local government structure. Each major function and each major service of the authority has its committee of elected members to review and deliberate the needs for that governmental activity and to propose policies which the council should adopt within that sphere of activity. There are two types of council committees: the functional committees responsible for broad aspects of local government operation such as finance, personnel, planning and coordination, policy and resources, and the service committees responsible for specific community services such as housing, education, public safety and social welfare.

Within this polycentric structure, each committee with its chairman, its subcommittees and its related department staffed by professional officers becomes a policy subsystem. Within its terms of reference, each functional or service committee in effect defines the policies, projects and programmes for that function or service. There may be formal delegation of powers from the council through standing orders, but, by convention, in actual practice committees are usually limited only by the applicable law and financing available (Maddick and Pritchard, 1958, p. 147; Greenwood et al., 1969a, p. 29). What each committee has done in its area of endeavour and which policies it wants to pursue are included in its reports to the council. Acceptance of its reports constitute council ratification.

The structure tends to make committee chairmanships into important powerful posts. The role of the chairman has evolved by custom and usage so that formal delegation of power is the exception rather than the rule. The various aspects of the chairman's role form critical links between the committees and their departments and with other council committees. In addition to keeping order and seeing that the work of the committee gets done, each chairman may generally be thought of as the committee's leader and representative within the system. As a leader, being informed and knowledgeable about the needs of the service is essential. Another part of the task is to see that officers provide sufficient information to the committee so that it can act on questions. He is the contact between officers and committee and is kept informed about requests to the department. Chairmen are usually empowered to act on routine matters referred to them by officers between regular committee meetings. As a representative, each chairman is the voice of his committee. The language of minutes and reports is subject to the chairman's approval. In the council and in consultation with other committees, the chairman is the committee spokesman. The chairman's most important representational task is his membership of functional committees such as finance or policy and resources. In party-controlled authorities, the chairman represents the committee majority in the party group (The Committee on the Management of Local Government, 1967b, pp. 153-6, 168). Senior experienced councillors tend to be appointed chairmen, although in party-controlled authorities there are additional tests. Chairmanships of functional committees tend to be reserved for party leaders in those authorities, while non-party councils lean towards seniority, personalities and leaders of factions.

The functional committees provide the means for linking the different committee subsystems together, and to some extent they supervise and control all authority activities. The finance committee, for example, reviews the budget requests of service committees and makes recommendations to the council for funding allocations. The establishment or personnel committee examines requests for new positions and staffing requirements for the services. General purposes or planning and coordination committees attempt to deal with questions of community development, joint programmes of services and areas of endeavour which may not fit neatly into a specific committee's sphere of work. In a limited fashion, functional committees act as coordinators of authority activities and services. New departures, programmes and projects are to some extent controllable through the power of the purse. New positions or added staffing require not only establishment approval but also money for salaries. Where a proposed activity is thought desirable, it can be supported. Where change is not deemed imperative, it can be delayed by denying funds or by allocating a smaller amount than requested. Where two committees propose to make provision for complementary services to the same or similar clientele, funding can be given with the understanding that it must become a joint venture. Coordination is mainly achieved through the use of negative powers, i.e. through the ability of functional committees, particularly the finance committee, to reject service committee requests. More often than not, coordination occurs because the chairmen of these controlling committees, invariably the leaders of the majority party, have decided to have coordination (The Committee on the Management of Local Government, 1967b, pp. 212–3).

## The Policy and Resources·Committee

Changes have been taking place in the committee system in many parts of the country since the mid-1960s. These changes have provided opportunity for greater control and coordination. The lengthy study and discussion of reorganization was paralleled by examinations of how local government might be made more effective. To this end both the Maud and Bains Committees recommended reductions in the numbers of council committees by combining tasks of service committees and by creating a single functional committee to formulate authority objectives and to coordinate the committee structure in their achievement. Maud designated this committee the management board, while Bains (in a modification of Maud proposals) named it the policy and resources committee. The former appeared to favour leadership control, while the modification was in the direction of achieving coordination through service committee participation in objective-setting.

While no common pattern for revised structures has yet emerged, the trends are in the directions indicated as desirable in the two reports. The traditional major committees remain the backbone of the structure: social services, housing, education, establishment, etc. Some minor committees have been eliminated and their tasks taken on by major committees with closely related concerns, e.g. placing libraries and museums under education. Elimination of council seats at reorganization fostered not only reduction in the numbers of committees but also in the size of the committees. Use of a functional committee for coordination of the committee structure and authority policies has become accepted practice. In many instances this has been accomplished by establishing a policy and resources committee, while in others it has meant combining policy oversight with finance or adding this function to the tasks of a general-purposes committee. Most Outer London boroughs, about a fourth of the county boroughs and about a third of the counties had policy and resources committees in 1969, according to studies by the Institute of Local Government Studies at Birmingham University.

Nearly all policy and resources committees have been placed into existing structures and procedures rather than simply being added on. This has meant taking over some of the tasks of finance and other committees concerned with resource allocation. Budget-making processes and decisions on expenditures, for example, may be handled by the policy committee, and finance in effect becomes a service committee that controls distribution of funds and accounts. Where a planning and coordination committee may have been responsible for the acquisition and use of land by the council, a subcommittee of policy and resources may now be responsible for land use with general resource planning activity absorbed by the main policy and resources committee. Although authorities rejected the Maud proposals for policy and resources committees with power to set objectives for all authority activities and to review the progress of committees towards those objectives, many policy committees have established planning procedures which ensure that long-range objectives, proposals and programmes of the services come under their scrutiny (Greenwood et al., 1971, pp. 165-6). Thus, while service committees tend to retain control over policy-making for the services and tend still to have responsibility for development of the service, their funding and future plans are subject to policy committee approval.

These trends are illustrated by changes which have taken place in the six authorities studied. All have to some extent modified their committee structures by reductions in the number of committees through recombination. Each has installed a policy and resources committee. One was established pre-Maud, the other five between 1967 and 1970. In two counties and two Outer London boroughs, policy and resources consists of a main committee and several subcommittees for such functions as finance, personnel, land, planning and coordination. The other two authorities have only the main committee, appointing *ad hoc* subcommittees for special tasks such as for development of recommendations on land use policies or for preparation of the estimates. The preeminent function for all six is considered to be control of finances and the budget-making process. As the Conservative chairman of one said, 'We deal with the resources of the authority—money, personnel and land—but our main task is to be the governor on the flywheel of funding.' All six have reviewed land questions on a case-by-case basis; none has evolved overall policies, and service committees such as education retain control of their land and its uses. Only one policy committee has ventured into long-range planning following the Bains model for service committee participation. These plans are mostly shelved owing to uncertainties of the economy, central government funding and high costs of committee requests.

As might be expected, members of these policy and resources committees are council leaders and chairmen of major committees such as education, social services, housing, finance and establishment. In these party-controlled authorities, there is absolute domination by the majority party with only 2 to 6 seats allotted to opposition parties. These seats are usually filled by minority leaders and shadow chairmen. Rank-and-file councillors do not figure in the make-up of two committees, are appointed only to subcommittees in three authorities and constitute about one-third of the membership in one authority. Generally, rank-and-file councillors are appointed from the majority party.

The potential power of policy and resources committees which emerges from their installation at the top of the structure has yet to be realized. However, having allocative functions centred in essentially one committee considerably reduces the polycentric nature of the committee system. When combined with party political control, there are multiple opportunities for controlling and shaping the policy process through decisions by the policy and resources committee. There is a certain ambivalence about affecting service committees' roles, particularly those such as education, which have traditionally enjoyed great degrees of freedom on delegation from the council. This ambivalence will be explored later. Again it illustrates that the achievement of coordination and control depends on the willingness of the majority leadership to use their domination of policy and resources committees for those ends.

### The Chief Executive's Advisory Board

Concomitant with the creation of policy and resources committees has been the advent of chief executives' advisory boards or management teams. Each authority in this study has its own arrangements, but the typical board consists of the treasurer, the director of planning, the chief officers of the 'spending' services such as education, social welfare and housing, and is chaired by the head of the authority's paid service, the chief executive. The purpose is to bring together the views of these specialists for consolidation into general perspectives on authority problems with the objective of coordination. Advisory boards do not work to policy and resources committees, although their discussions are an aid to the chief executives who do. Nor have these boards undertaken the task of reviewing and giving opinions on requests or policy recommendations of individual services. Most of their activities have been directed towards the administrative side by examining ways of helping departments in implementing authority-wide policies such as those for land use or joint facilities. Some have gone into the area of interservice coordination in projects such as when housing provision and recreation amenities are to be included in the redevelopment of a high street shopping precinct. These activities may result in the issue of a report as an administrative guide for the departments' reference. In a few cases, advisory teams have carried out performance reviews of departments, at the request of their chief officers, as aids to the improvement of their management techniques.

There is an uncertainty about these management teams and their emerging roles which is focused about changing power relationships. Officers appear to prefer the type of coordination which is brought about through a service committee's interactions with policy and resources, e.g. through political mechanisms. Given the relative separateness of each committee, this may be another way of saying that everyone wants coordination but no one wants to be coordinated, at least not by their peers. At the administrative level, discussion and cooperation among departments have been normal activities in local governments. However, the installation of the chief executive as *primus inter pares* has brought about the potential for a new centre of power within the structure. The result has been that other officers have taken a cautious approach to a limited range of problems through these boards or teams. It seems evident that advisory boards of chief executives will not have clearly defined roles until policy and resources committees have sorted out their own uses of power and until they decide to place advisory and executive functions with management teams.

## The Education Committee

Education as a local government activity is controlled by the council through its education committee. Under the 1944 Act, local education authorities are required to appoint an education committee, the composition of which is subject to approval by the Secretary of State. There must be a majority of elected members as well as places for coopted members, i.e. persons experienced and interested in education. Coopted members generally include church representatives and, increasingly, teacher representatives and members of home–school associations. The size of education committees varies widely owing largely to circumstances of history and community development. The smallest committee in the six authorities studied was 24 plus 12 coopted members in an Outer London borough; the largest was in a county authority, 61 plus 20 coopted members. In all three counties, membership was reduced 6 to 10 places at reorganization with coopted members often bearing the brunt of the reduction.

Education committees tend to spawn a large number of subcommittees owing to both heavy workload and multiple areas of responsibility within the service. Policy development and oversight of activities within the sphere of each subcommittee is delegated to it by the main committee. The two most usual divisions of labour are by the various sections of the service (primary, secondary and further education, adult education and youth service, administration including finance and, perhaps, buildings) and by the functions of the service (schools, further and technical education, finance and policy, sites and buildings, planning and development). Occasionally, there are further subdivisions for special activities or for examination of particular questions of a somewhat continuing nature, e.g. ROSLA, nursery provision.

Coordination of this array of subcommittees is necessary to ensure that existing policies are followed and that emerging policies do not conflict with current policy or other policy proposals. There is also the necessity of devising a budget for the service and of monitoring expenditures or requests for supplementary spending by the various branches. Where there are few subcommittees, the main committee may find it feasible to act as the coordinating body. Where there are five or more subcommittees, one is often designated to carry out the coordinating task. The name used usually describes the role: planning and coordination, policy and finance, coordination and development. They are usually made up of the subcommittee chairmen, the chairman and the vice-chairman of the main committee as well as other members. Occasionally, the coordinating subcommittee consists of chairmen only. Of the six authorities, one county uses the main committee to coordinate, although there are *ad hoc* meetings of chairmen from time to time. The other five authorities have coordinating subcommittees, but none are made up exclusively of chairmen.

The bulk of work is done in subcommittees, while the main committee is inclined to be a forum for debate and discussion. Reports received from the subcommittees are approved by the full committee, usually with one word 'agreed', and are sent on to the council as the report of the education committee. Where there are differences of opinion between factions or parties or where there is some difficulty about the impact of a recommendation, questions will be raised and perhaps a vote will be taken. The lack of argumentation and displays of partisanship in education committee sessions is often attributed to the fact that its meetings are open to the public and the press, making such actions unseemly. In reality the subcommittee system contributes a great deal to the rather cut and dried atmosphere of the main committee meetings by providing places for effective discussion lower down the policy subsystem. Another factor is the non-controversial nature of most agenda items, e.g. routine expenditures for maintenance of buildings, transportation, setting of hours for recreational use of school grounds and accounting of children with special educational needs. Of course, councillors have their own views on what is non-controversial and what is not. How educational interests become political issues and how they are handled through the policy process will be examined shortly.

## The Education Department

It is essential to describe the department in relation to the education committee because of the role it plays in providing professional expertise in the policy-making process. As the administrative arm of the service, headed by the chief education officer, the department's purposes are to manage the service in accordance with authority policies, to evaluate its effectiveness and to advise the education committee on future development and policy. The department is a communications hub, responding daily to the concerns of parents, members of the public, heads and teachers. It attends to a myriad of administrative details and handles the questions of governors, councillors, the treasurer's office and the chief executive's staff. These contacts keep the department's hand on the pulse of the system, and they yield information useful to the department in carrying out its purposes. Principal officers are almost invariably educators selected for their knowledge and competence in the field in order to provide the authority with professional advice and technical skills. While the bulk of the department's time and effort is taken up by the routines of management, the most important functions of officers revolve around their interactions with the education committee.

The dominance of the committee system is reflected in the organization of the education department. Under the direction of the chief education officer, the deputy or each of the deputies and assistant education officers supervise and manage some particular branch of the service. For example, a deputy may look after financial matters, coordinating them within the department for schools and other branches, and he may conduct the relationships with the authority treasurer's department. This deputy would most likely work to a subcommittee on administration and finance. An assistant officer might have charge of the schools section and would work to the schools subcommittee. The chief education officer invariably takes the coordinating subcommittee and the main committee, although most officers attend meetings of the latter *en banc*. These organizational arrangements vary with committee structure and size of the department, but in general it may be said that the more critical areas such as finance, development and coordination are handled by the top tier of officers. When special questions of a somewhat continuous nature arise, such as the planning of a building programme or secondary reorganization, and need to be considered by a subcommittee or an *ad hoc* committee, it is often the chief education officer who is initially involved.

Chief education officers have two important links with the education committee: the chairman and written reports to the committee. In both the objective is facilitating the exchange of information and ideas. How each is handled is, however, very much dictated by the administrative style of the chief education officer and the expectations of the chairman. At minimum, the chief education officer sees to it that the chairman has sufficient knowledge of current business and emerging problems to run an effective meeting or to respond to his requests on matters arising between meetings. More ideally, a close continuous relationship is developed, through which each has an understanding of the other's role and the constraints on that role in given situations. As for report writing, some chief education officers view it as an art form, through which facts can be transmitted within a context of professional thought about needs and questions. For others, report writing is a chore that must be done, and far more can be accomplished by conversational presentation and discussion. This topic of information exchange between professionals and politicians will be explored more fully in a later chapter as it is a critical element in the policy process.

Within the education department, coordination at the officer level is essential given the division of responsibilities by sections and subcommittees. In part, coordinative activities concern management problems and matters connected with schools and personnel. However, much of what is in need of coordination is the information and recommendations that go to committees and the kinds of decisions that are required from them. The means of achieving coordination vary from department to department but is usually centred in meetings of officers under the direction of the chief education officer. The size of the group, its designation and frequency of meeting differ from place to place, but the functions of each are about the same as those listed by one chief education officer: to inform and consult colleagues on policy problems, to give feedback on political situations, to reach decisions on items involving two or more officers and committees, to resolve conflicts between officers or between the department and schools, to report on relationships with other departments. The authorities studied have the following arrangments for such sessions. Two Outer London boroughs hold weekly meetings consisting of the four or five principal officers and the chief education officer. In one, it is formally known as the directorate, in the other the staff meeting. The third holds what the CEO calls office staff meetings as needed during the committee cycle, calling in those officers concerned with particular questions. In the county authorities, the meeting groups tend to be larger, six to eighteen officers and others. In one authority this is the directorate, in the other two the cabinet. All three usually meet once regularly during the cycle. There are, as will be seen, less formal coordinative mechanisms, each authority having evolved its own patterns of office consultation.

This section has outlined the committee structure of local government and has identified several linking roles of the chairmen and the functional and coordinating committees within it. The next section examines the impact of party political control on the structure through the conversion of these chairmanships and committees to points for the exercise of political control. The implications of this conversion for policy-making and for officers' roles are introduced.

## Political Control in Local Government

The committee system of local government operates in a framework of political influence, activity and struggle for its control. Local government in England, like many other governments, was not designed with organized political parties in mind. In the absence of organized parties, localism dominates its politics: community sectionalism, social class differences, old versus new residents, low rates ideology versus maximization of services—all these provide foci for the cliques and factions which struggle for control. The trend towards party politics is replacing the politics of localism, and approaches to questions as well as policy solutions proposed tend to be tested against party philosophies and benefits to the parties as well as community benefit. Because political parties have their own purposes to fulfil in seeking and taking control of the processes of local government, they bring the influence of their values and principles to bear on the conduct of local affairs. Through the application of party programme to local problems, a party hopes to become identified with effectiveness in governing. This identification increases its influence; the result is that the party gains office and continues in office.

There are advantages and disadvantages to party political control of government. Because it is organized around sets of principles, a party tends to provide greater consistency in approaches to problems. However, this may lead to doctrinaire solutions rather than to pragmatic answers based on full assessment of local conditions. It may also lead to cautious approaches or sudden swings in policy direction if control alternates between two parties. Party control may mean more rapid action on community needs but, perhaps, at the cost of wide consultation and discussion. Where two or more parties, exist, one is always ready to point out faults in the proposals of the other(s). While this can lead to greater ranges of alternatives and possibly can result in beneficial compromises, it might lead to the hardening of positions especially if manoeuvring for political advantage is detected as a prime motivation. Electoral contests between parties can provide the electorate with some better formulated ideas of what government should do and perhaps a clear choice between policies to be pursued. However, electors can at least choose the party most compatible with their personal views or which in their judgement has the better record of previous service.

Perhaps the most basic implication that party political control holds for local government is its effect on the locus of decision-taking within the committee system. Table 3 has been devised to illustrate the tendencies which seem to emerge as party political control evolves. It is based on the Maud Committee findings about committees and administration (The Committee on the Management of Local Government, 1967a) and Bulpitt's (1967) research on party politics in local councils. The Maud material stressed the roles of committees, chairmen and officers and also where decisions were made under differing circumstances of non-party and party control. It was concluded that in non-party authorities chairmen and officers tend to make the decisions, while committees endorse decisions. In party-controlled councils, a majority party and its party group hold 'the reality of power', and, if that power is used 'toughly', the role of committees is diminished (The Committee on the Management of Local Government, 1967, p. 114). Moreover, the power of chairmen tends to be reduced, and officers' influence is constrained by party programme. Bulpitt was interested in the effects of party on council activity, the implications for council leadership and the influence of officers. The results of his study indicated that two interactive factors were important in the determination of the style of politics in councils: organization of

## Table 3: Tendencies in Political Control and Local Government Policy-Making Control

| | Independents[a] and small local parties | Independent majority, scattering of local parties and few national party members | National party shares majority with Independents or local party | National party in majority vs. weakly organized opposition of one or two national parties, few Independents | National party in majority vs. strongly organized opposition of another national party | Strongly organized national party in majority vs. organized opposition of another national party |
|---|---|---|---|---|---|---|
| Party make-up of council | | | | | | |
| **Policy-making control: Informal** | Personalities, cliques, leaders of factions and groups | Faction and party leaders in weak alliances | Temporary alliances of party leaders and influential members | Party group and/or influential members of majority | Majority leader and influential members of majority or party group | Majority party group and party policy advisory committee |
| Formal | Full council | Full council and/or ad hoc joint committees | Full council and/or finance committee, policy and resources committee | Majority. controlled policy and resources committee and full council | Majority controlled policy and resources committee | Policy and resources committee possibly of majority members only |
| **Roles of committees: Functional** | Decide allocations with reference to their own perceptions of service's needs and committee's influence | Negotiate allocations with some consultation by service committee chairmen and leaders | Allocations decided on basis of policy proposals by committees, consultation with influentials, party leaders | Allocations made reflect majority policy as interpreted through service committee chairmen | Follow majority policy on allocations and oversee use by service committee | Follow majority policy on allocations, monitor service committees' uses rigorously |

| Service | Co-administrator of service with chief officer | Co-administrator of service with chairman and chief officer | Co-administrator of service with chairman and chief officer—ratify policies recommended | Political defender of service with the majority; may make party policies for service | Develop suggested policies largely in line with majority party views | Political arm of service; policy watchdog for the majority party |
|---|---|---|---|---|---|---|
| Roles of committee chairmen | Represent service in council | 'Mini-minister' for service within council | 'Mini-minister' for service with leaders and other committees | Political advisor to chief officer and committee; speaks for service in the majority party | Party policy advisor to committee; political advisor to chief officer | Political advisor to chief officer, party policy interpreter to committee majority; service spokesmen in party |
| Department and chief officers, relationships to committee | Policy-maker for service | Policy-maker for service; advisor to chairman | Policy-recommender *cum* policy-maker to committee; advisor to chairman | Policy-recommender and advisor to committee | Policy-recommender to chairman; political filter for service (shared task with chairman) | Policy-recommender and advisor to chairman and committees |
| Time | some ── tendency ── to ── develop ── over ── time ── towards ── organized ── party ── control | | | | | |

<sup>a</sup> Independents are defined as non-party non-aligned but essentially apolitical members and aggregates. In later stages they may be considered as an antisocialist bloc.

the council (e.g. taking chairmanships) and party cohesiveness and discipline (e.g. taking group decisions, applying group sanctions). The greater is the discipline of one party, the greater the partisanship and the less the emphasis on interpersonal relationships among the leaders. It was also pointed out that, when one party (particularly the majority party) becomes more disciplined, other parties or factions tend to react with a hardening of their own discipline (Bulpitt, 1967, pp. 99, 110–11). The implication for officers' influence was that it tended to decline as partisanship increased.

Thus, when a council has a large proportion of local parties and Independents (defined as non-party affiliated, non-aligned aggregates and individuals) the tendency is towards a polycentric system in which functional and service committees interpret their own terms of reference. Resource allocation by the finance committee is highly dependent on its views of local needs. Service committees have few checks on their decisions and tend to give a good deal of attention to the details of administration. This situation can give rise to committee empires and to chairmen acting as so-called 'mini-ministers' in representing their services with other committees and the council. Accomodation of differences and settling of disputes is done by factional leaders or influential personalities, occasionally extending into council meetings. Chief officers' technical competence and day-to-day responsibilities in running the services tends to make them *de facto* policy-makers for their services.

Election of council members by parties and organization of committees by the majority tends to deemphasize factions and personalities. The orientation and tasks of functional and service committees begin to change as the political dimensions of their activities become increasingly critical to party performance. Their decisions become more preconditioned to party policy and programme and subject to party approval. The council has less final control over policy, and many decisions about handling policy proposals are made either through a functional committee consisting of influential members of the majority or informally through the majority party group. Chairmen become political advisors to their chief officers, and each officer tends to recommend polices which can be more or less rationalized within his chairman's perceptions of, and influence in, his party.

When parties are strongly organized, e.g. when they take all chairmanships, when they adhere to group decisions, when they use the whip in the council, when they apply group sanctions, etc., there is a tendency towards more centralization of decision-taking. The majority party group exercises a high degree of control over the decisions made. Their control is extended into the committee structure through their leadership's domination of functional committees, especially policy and resources. Service committee majorities propose policies in line with party philosophy aims and programmes. Chairmen tend to monitor and control majority members to ensure that proposals meet with party approval. They are usually advocates and spokesmen for their services in the party group although subject to group decisions. In this situation, chairmen are political advisors to chief officers, keeping them informed of party desires and directions. Chief officers, in turn, recommend policy from their professional technical knowledge while working closely with chairmen and, perhaps, majority members for political guidance. Chief officers also act as political filters for their departments, keeping subordinates abreast of changing political situations.

Clearly, increased party political control of local councils tends to mean an increased centralization of decision-taking in policy matters, a decrease in the control and administration of services by committees and a shift in emphasis of committee chairmen's roles from service representatives to political spokesmen and advisors. Party groups and party leaders, through their control of policy and resources and other functional committees, become more critical as participants and decision-makers for all services and activities. The technical competence of chief officers as bases for policy proposals is increasingly accompanied by a competence in tailoring recommendations within given political boundaries.

These are only tendencies, and individual authorities may very owing to the particular history of the community, the degree of control the majority party feels it can exercise without adverse repercussions and the behaviour of other parties in the reaction to majority proposals. Individual councillors may still exert special influence in party-controlled authorities, but it will more likely derive from their place in the party and collectable political debts than personality. Chief officers may be found who have greater influence than might be expected under party domination, based not on professional expertise but on political perspicacity.

The six authorities in this study showed marked degrees of party political control and centralization of policy-making. Each of the three Outer London boroughs was controlled by a strongly organized national party, one Labour, two Conservative, and they all faced organized party opposition. Policy development and committee roles were closely regulated through the majority party group. The counties were more variable. In the rual county a national party, the Conservatives, shared control with the Independents. Policy-making control tended to reside with party leaders in the absence of a majority group. Committees were beginning to withdraw from administering services and were increasingly expected by the leaders to develop policy recommendations. The other two counties had national party majorities, one Conservative, one Labour, each with a somewhat weakly organized opposition. In the Labour-controlled county, the opposition was a Conservative–Independent antisocialist coalition. Although policy control was exercised through the majority party group in both authorities, influential members tended to be more important in the Labour group, while the Conservative group tended to be dominated by one leader. Roles of service committees were inclined towards developing a policy in line with group aims more than towards making a policy which would later be given a party imprimatur.

This is the larger frame of party political control. The exercise of control is conditioned by party approaches to local government and its implementation through the party group; these are topics to be examined next.

*Political Parties*

There was a surge of party politics into local government following the Second World War, and over the following two decades it stabilized with about half of all councils being organized by parties. The increases in party control over local councils that came with reorganization in 1974 has extended party politics into nearly all counties and metropolitan districts of England. The Labour Party has a long history of interest in local government and controlled a number of boroughs before coming to power at Westminster for the first time in 1924. The

Conservative Party, sometimes under local labels including Independent and rate-payers, has had increasing influence in councils since the 1940s. This has not usually been direct influence in terms of taking control but rather it lends an outlook or philosophy as a rallying point for antisocialist sentiment. As reorganization became a greater certainty, the Conservatives more frequently organized and vied for control under the party banner. The renewed Liberal Party began its drive for national power in the 1960s by seeking local bases through campaigning for community politics and action. It has avoided the use of a party label where there were 'true' Independents in order to emphasize this community orientation and to heighten its brand of political identity.

The use of political labels, particularly national party labels, helps council members to define themselves and each other. Often the identification is made in terms of the national party and its position on national questions. Additionally, each party has its own outlook on local government and how it should be conducted under the party's philosophy for facing societal concerns. How each party looks at specific social services such as education may be presumed from this, as well as from the stands each takes on related issues in Parliament. Individual adherence to party views may seem to be loose, but most members tend to believe that they are firmly anchored to the basic principles of the party whose label they take. How a member identifies himself may sometimes be made on the basis of exception such as when an Independent says he is an anti-socialist. While a party label at the local level offers some clues as to the way a member and his colleagues may act in the council, it is more important as an indicator of principles to which he is committed. Therefore, in describing a party's outlook on local government, elected members from that party are also described as to their orientations.

For Labour, caucus, work and discipline exemplify its approach to local government as another sphere in which to advance socialist principles. The party group and the party as a whole should have an influence on policy (Newton, 1973, p. 301). While there are doctrinal differences within the party, members tend to coalesce around principles that have to do with concern for the majority of people and the betterment of the under-privileged and working classes and that stand for humaneness and equality (Locke, 1974, p. 8). These are vague ideals but, as one councillor said, 'Labour is a vehicle, a way of getting from here to there, but you have to accept a broad definition of "there" to get us all in.' Getting there is also very much a matter of how, and the party group often specifies this aspect for members, particularly for committee chairmen (Kogan, 1973, pp. 40-3). On education, Labour tends to make more generous provision, attempts to reach more lower-class people by extending opportunity, tries to remove barriers to educational progress for individuals and, perhaps, shows more concern for education than for other local services (Boaden, 1971, p. 31; Kogan, 1973, pp. 151-2). Often, Labour is criticized for its haste in pursuing aims set by doctrine and conditioned by ideals without examining alternative solutions. The following story may be apocryphal, but it is illustrative. Once, in a solid working-class Labour-controlled borough the chief education officer brought in a plan for phasing in comprehensives and phasing out the eleven-plus, one school at a time. 'Can you begin making these changes in all the schools at the same time?' asked the majority leader. The chief education officer allowed that it could be done with some more planning. 'Then that is the way we'll do it,' replied the leader, 'for, when we rise, we all rise together.'

The Conservative Party believes that parties make two contributions to local government: organization and a known body of principle. Organization is not party discipline but rather a way of keeping antisocialist forces together. Principles are guides to action on issues which provide sufficient bases and directions in making decisions (The Conservative Party Centre, 1969, pp. 7-9). At the centre of Conservative principles are ideas of minimum government interference in peoples' lives and the market place as well as caution and fiscal prudence when it does seem necessary to have governmental intervention. Party members in the council arrive at a policy not necessarily on the basis of what the larger party organization propounds but rather on what elected members believe they should do according to principle. Individual councillors are supposedly free of the party group and free to interpret these principles for themselves. This indicates some incipient factionalism, a distinction between those who interpret principles for application to actual situations and those who strictly adhere to them as concepts. The differences are detectable, as noted by the chief education officer in an authority long controlled by the Conservatives, 'In the recent election, some "high Tories" were returned, determined to trim expenditures and to stop education from its social levelling. They say they are non-political in this, but there are clear ties to strict Tory viewpoints.' In education, the Conservatives tend to support freedom of choice, an academic tradition, and assume that there is a limited pool of talent from which society's leaders can be drawn through progression up the educational ladder (Locke, 1974, p. 8). This has led some people to conclude that the Conservatives want an elite education for some predestined elite. As a local education interest group leader said, 'As a national party, the Conservatives want to keep societal differences fostered by different secondary schools and by selection at eleven-plus.' However, party attitude is difficult to define. Edward Boyle, when Education Minister, spoke of the inability to divide children through selection practices, and the 1966 party manifesto indicated that reorganization of secondary education was not a bad thing but that going comprehensive should be opposed if haste was put ahead of soundness in planning (Lewin, 1968, pp. 140-1). A number of councillors interviewed in this study gave similar responses and often focused on the notion that Labour always wants to move too fast. There were also Conservative councillors 'absolutely opposed to the destruction of our grammar schools'.

Independents are difficult to define as part of the party political galaxy. When considered as an antisocialist element, it is relatively easy to 'lump' them with the Conservatives. When organized around some aspect of local concern as rate-payers' groups often are, then Independents may be defined as a local party. However, independent Independents who follow no national party principles, who do not utilize group decision-making and who want committee chairmanships and council leadership responsibilities shared out on a non-party basis do not seem to belong in a classification of parties (Beith, 1972, pp. 288-9). One Independent leader summed it up well, 'I am an Independent, because I don't think politics has any place in local government. The wrong decisions are taken when people follow political dogma. It intrudes on good sense.' Essentially, then, Independents may be classified as apolitical. Yet, in this study it was found that Independents in two county authorities were aligned with the Conservatives. In the third county, though working closely with the Conservatives, the Independents seemed to be well-organized, politically astute and working hard to blunt the political power of both major parties.

In addition to being apolitical, Independents tend to be fiscal conservatives. Moderation in setting the rates is a central theme. Socioeconomic well-being of the community and maintenance of essential services are paramount. The concept of local government as an administrator of national government policies is accepted as the limited role of the council. These principles extend into education. It is a service to be provided, and, if central government policy is to go comprehensive, Independents believe that there is no alternative and no room for political waffling. However, in the absence of additional rate support funds, they believe any mandates in education should proceed only as each authority can find the funds and not in accordance with some timetable set at Westminster. While Independents would like the needs and desires of the community to be put first in deciding educational provision as well as in considering other services, they feel that community considerations no longer carry weight with the Department of Education and Science nor with major parties in the local councils.

The Liberal Party, revived on a national scale, is also difficult to classify in local politics. The call to community politics and action proclaimed by the Liberals tends to put the spotlight on local questions and the involvement of people: local solutions are better than national mandates. There are exceptions, however, when national policy may be needed to protect the weak from the powerful. Party organization is important, especially if the other major parties are organized. However, binding group decisions are to be avoided, and group meetings should be devoted to exchanges of information and ideas (The Liberal Party, 1960, p. 9). Liberals seem free to decide with whom they will work in local government. If alliances with other parties or Independents will advance the Liberal cause, then such alliances are allowable. In this study, Liberals were found to have their own three-member group in one authority, one Liberal was attached to the Independent group in another authority and in a third authority, one Liberal apparently meets with Labour, while his three colleagues seem to act individually. On education, Liberals seem to follow their general principles. Comprehensives are not entirely bad, but their installation in an authority should have the endorsement of the people; at the same time, grammar schools should not be eliminated as long as there are people who want to choose that type of school for their youngsters. More money for education is necessary in all localities, and central government should find ways of providing it for less wealthy authorities while compelling well-off communities to put more of their own money into education. This may seem confusing to some, but Liberal councillors can apparently keep it straight. As one said, 'Comprehensives have proved to be good schools here. Reorganization is expensive, but this authority can afford it for the 50 or 60% of the people who want it. However, the Tory majority keeps telling the people that grammar schools are better for them.'

*Party Groups*

While a party label helps to define members, it is the party group which defines the party in the local setting and in the council. Composed mainly of elected members, each group carries out four functions: to maintain contact with the larger party, to develop policy directions, to organize its members on the council and to determine how they are to proceed as a party in conducting council business. These things are accomplished through exchanges of information and ideas in a democratic fashion. However, as with any democratic organization there are tendencies toward oligarchy. Party leaders usually hold the group chairmanship and the majority of seats on the group executive or steering committee.

Contact with national party headquarters is usually maintained through the leaders. Labour is more organized about these contacts than the other parties, additionally designating members on major committees such as education in order to receive information and directives from Transport House. The Conservatives tend to rely more on regional arrangements, calling leaders in for discussion on central government actions and national party policies as they apply to local authorities. The Greater London region is covered quite intensely by both parties because of the added necessity of monitoring the actions of the Greater London Council. However, leaders of both major parties in all six authorities indicated that what is produced at national headquarters is freely rejected for local application if, in the words of one Conservative leader, '. . . it doesn't fit this county or our local philosophy'.

Locally, groups maintain continuous contact with their constituency parties and ward organizations. Labour has more formal structures for doing so, because the party constitution stipulates a number of critical decisions as the sole province of the ward meeting, e.g. selection of candidates to stand for the ward. Thus, there are often seats for ward representatives on the executive committee or group policy committee. These people can raise questions about the directions being taken in the council and can aid elected members in deciding party policies. In writing the party manifesto as election time approaches, the group proposes objectives and obtains reactions from the wards either through these representatives or from a party committee on local government, a constituencies' organization which includes elected members.

The Conservatives are beginning to emulate Labour in these aspects of local party contact. Increasingly there are *ad hoc* party committees composed of elected members and constituency representatives which try to overcome the traditional separateness of the constituency organizations. In one of the London authorities, ideas for the 1974 manifesto were gathered from the group's shadow chairmen by one energetic councillor, then they were tested with constituency representatives and finally they were sent to the leader by the group as a guide for preparing the election document. In previous years, the leader had written it by himself instead of going through the difficulties of negotiating with three disparate constituency organizations.

Development of local long-range party policies is another task for the groups. Party philosophy and manifestos are the guides, but the substance of policy thinking is usually limited to authority finances and the rates. Occasionally major issues such as housing and reorganization of secondary education are reexamined with the result that previous party stands are reaffirmed but updated to justify recent party actions, *post hoc*. If a thorny problem arises, it is turned over to the group executive or policy committee, e.g. the party leaders, for examination. They take up the task of devising a policy recommendation. Outside experts, often professionals who are party members, may be called in to advise. In one of the London boroughs, Labour's advisor on education is the headmaster in a school maintained by the authority and a long-time party stalwart. Similarly, in one of the county authorities, the Conservative group has a local officer of the National Association of Schoolmasters, a retired grammar school head and a teacher from another authority in its stable of advisors.

The frequency of policy planning sessions varies widely, although Labour groups in this study meet more faithfully than do the Conservatives. Four times a year seems to be the favourite scheduling of Labour while Tories tend towards once a year, if at all. The Conservative minority leader in one county thought his group last met to discuss policy directions about two years before reorganization. Party leaders indicate that there are two distinct difficulties in holding such meetings. First, most members do not want to think beyond the next council meeting and cannot be made to think beyond the next election. Immediate problems occupy their minds. Second, authority officers are not present to provide essential information and advice. Most officers follow the ethics of not attending one-party meetings. The result is that policy development is neglected except when it can be squeezed into group meetings that take place within the regular council meeting cycle.

The hard focus of party groups is on organizing their members in the council, on keeping abreast of committee actions and on deciding the stands that the party will take on developing issues. The organization task must be first as it is of prime importance in control if the party is in the majority and in making the most out of opposition if the party is in the minority. Committee memberships are generally assigned by party leaders on the basis of members' stated interests, experience and adherence to party philosophy. Labour often adds the element of party work. For example, a newly elected member has a better chance for a prime committee seat if he has previously stood as a sacrificial candidate in a Tory-dominated ward. Selection of chairmen or shadow chairmen is rarely left to chance—leaders submit names to the group and usually obtain the people they want. Of course, the group also decides who the leaders will be, and, in doing so, it sorts out any factional difficulties of the local party.

Election of group leaders is not difficult if there is no hurdle of factionalism to overcome. Conservatives lean towards experienced members, often choosing the most senior. Labour looks at experience, too, but with more emphasis on party service and committee posts held. Both parties will usually keep a leader in power as long as he wants provided he does not commit a major mistake, jeopardizing the party's future.

Factions are another matter and can bring on leadership struggles. Each party seems to deal with it in a different way. In one London borough, a 'young turk' faction of strict Tories in a preponderant Conservative majority tried to take over from the moderates. The group resolved the leadership contest by selecting a younger man somewhat to the right of centre, rejecting more senior members put up by each faction. The controlling Labour groups in two councils, a county and a borough, divided over how to use the power of the majority. The crisis in the county was partially an urban–rural split. A caucus, or clique, of about six experienced councillors from borough areas, controlling the group, could not convince new councillors from rural areas to accept their hard-handed approach. In the London borough, it was the younger, more aggressive middle-class Labourites seeking to displace cautious experienced working-class socialists. The result in both instances was to select two leaders, the challengers getting the majority leaders' posts, while the challenged faction took the group chairmanships.

Selection of chairmen and shadow chairmen is critical both for the leaders and the groups. In addition to the tests for committee membership, essential qualities are an ability to work with officers without being dominated by them and to keep applying the party line both in committee deliberations and when acting for the committee. A chairman who parrots his chief officer when reporting back to the group is obviously weak on both counts. He may find himself teamed with a strong vice-chairman or a few extra majority committee members if such difficulties are expected. The choice of chairmen and shadow chairmen has significance for control or opposition beyond the immediate committee work. The heading of functional committees such as finance, establishment and policy and resources is usually reserved for majority party leaders and experienced influential councillors. The membership of these committees is usually comprised of chairmen of major committees, the 'spending' committees, such as education, social services, housing, etc., with the minority leadership taking seats on the other side of the table. The group will usually give the leaders the chairmen or shadow chairmen that they want because party effectiveness will depend on their compatibility with the leaders.

Voting for chairmen or shadow chairmen is often the only voting performed in groups. Sometimes this is because there are disputes over sectional interests, e.g. urban versus rural. Often it is to settle factional disputes and to press through a change-over in leadership. The 'young turk' faction of strict Tories in the London borough followed its leadership victory by throwing out old-time chairmen because they were, as one turk put it, '. . . fuddy-duddy and not true blue (some were positively pink)'; thus every chairmanship and vice-chairmanship was voted on ' . . . far into the night'. In two county councils where Independents are allied in a majority with Conservatives, all major committee chairmanships went to Conservatives, even though Independents hold the balance of power in each council. In one there have been no group meetings of Independents or Conservatives since they organized the council, according to the chairman of the policy and resources committee and the nominal leader of the majority.

What to do and which stands to take is decided in groups prior to the council meeting. There is usually a report by the leadership on items previously left with the executive or policy committee. If the party is in the majority, items may be referred to the policy and resources or the appropriate service committees. The council agenda is reviewed with each committee chairman or shadow chairman being responsible for leading discussion on the committee report and recommendations. If the group feels that some particular item is not ready for council action or does not square with party policy, they mark it for referral back to the committee or for withdrawal for group consideration. For the majority party, this process is easy; for the minority, it is impossible unless the leader can reach a procedural arrangement with the majority leader. Each party decides how reports will be treated, assigns speakers and gives notice of motions to be put forward in the council.

In two authorities, the minority groups, one Labour, one Conservative, holds 'off-monthly' meetings. In these sessions, close attention is given to committee activities and proposals. The purpose is twofold: to see what can be done about the directions being taken by committees and to determine what will be coming up in the policy and resources committee. Often discussion is confined to developments on major issues or in one or two committees. The outcomes are frequently used for establishing party policy and for furthering party strategy in line with existing policy.

Before discussing party discipline as fostered by the groups, it is essential to note the variations in quality and effectiveness of group meetings. There is a high degree of dependence on the leaders to point out issues, to indicate directions and to keep bickering to a minimum if effectiveness is to be achieved. Chairmen or shadow chairmen must provide information with candour if quality is to be attained. These conditions were more likely to be met in the groups which held the majority in the council, even though three of them had recently undergone the blood-letting of factional disputes. Among the groups of minority parties, three of the four Labour groups also met these conditions. The other was in trouble because the shadow chairmen, many of them new to county government, were not getting sufficient information to the group. One of the two Conservative groups in the minority was in the most difficulty. According to several members, group meetings consisted of ' . . . a monologue by our leader, followed by members' backbiting comments that committee shadow chairman are letting the socialists put too many things over on them'.

Discipline and use of the whip also varies from group to group. Party positions are established by a consensus and, occasionally, by votes of the group. These decisions are taken after discussion of the issue and the acceptable alternatives in relation to party aims and principles. Members are expected to abide by group decisions in the committees and in the council, although excuses may be granted. Conservatives say that they allow conscience and violation of constituents' wishes as excuses. According to one leader, for Labour members ' . . . it is best to be absent with an iron-clad reason'. All six Labour groups use the whip in the council on all matters, with five leaving it to committee chairmen or shadow chairmen to decide on using the whip for committee votes. However, on a major issue this becomes a leadership decision based on an assessment of group discussions and an estimate of what other parties might do on the issue. Three of the five Conservative groups use the whip in the council on organization matters and, occasionally, on issues in committees. The latter seems to be strictly a leadership decision and not a chairman's decision. In the other two groups, there is ' . . . no need to use the whip as each member knows the party's principles and the group's views'. Use of the whip by Conservatives seems to be on the increase, and members object to this incursion on their freedom to act. However, they say that it must be so, because Labour uses the whip on so many issues.

Use of the whip in local councils has a bad name which seems undeserved. Criticism centres on the fact that local government is not like Parliament where the majority can lose control of the government if it loses a key vote. There is also some feeling that it might be different if all councillors were allowed free votes. The first criticism misses the point. A show of solidarity is an end in itself, especially for Labour groups. On difficult issues, a group decision by Labour is enforced in order to demonstrate group and party responsibility for the action. The second criticism has some merit, particularly if there is factionalism in a party. Labour can often expect abstentions at the ideological extremes even after a full group discussion. Therefore, after the majority has decided, the whip is used to tie in the loose ends. Adherence to a new interpretation of party principles often has to be enforced by a group decision and the whip after a leadership struggle. Sometimes, when they are allied in a majority with Independents, the whip is necessary for the Conservatives on issues where individual Independents may disagree. To maintain control over issues is important for any majority party and its image of effective government. For Conservatives, it may be becoming more important than the image of individual freedom to dissent from group decisions. As one councillor noted, 'Ten years ago we voted our consciences without interference by the leader. Now, for public purposes, he likes to see all his troops facing the same way.'

## Summary

The introduction to the local education authority as a policy centre listed the powers and duties of local authorities under the Education Act of 1944, indicating the breadth of policy-making areas with which members and officers are concerned. The central feature of local government, its polycentric committee system, was described next. The responsibilities of the functional committees, including the policy and resources committee, were considered to be control and coordination; the relationships with the service committees were also indicated. The organization of the education department, under the direction of the chief education officer emphasized its parallelism with the committee structure for the service. To complete the picture, these elements were then set in the political frame of parties and the imperatives of control.

The political frame of local government is increasingly being provided by organized political parties. They bring party philosophies, principles and points of view to bear on council operations, Elected members and the local party undeniably reorient party views for application to local problems, and, in doing this, they define the party in the community. The result is that a party which achieves a majority control is identified with certain stands and directions in local government and on social issues. These become criteria or guides against which councillors, committees and officers can judge policy proposals for party acceptability. Proposals are screened and modified for a best fit against party templates, and argumentation develops around how to achieve party aims. Other criteria such as community need, costs and potential benefits are not ignored but have to take their place alongside party considerations in an approximate ordering of aims, impacts and priorities.

Political action centres on the party groups, especially the majority party group. It is a focal point for power and decisions about policies and the policy-making process. The committee structure of local government is most amenable to party political control. By organizing the council, by taking a majority of seats on each committee, by designating chairmen and by placing its leaders at the head of functional committees, a party in the majority greatly enhances its opportunities for implementing the party programme. Monitoring, directing and exercising control is a task of the party group. Airing opinions and exchanging information and ideas, thus leading to group decisions, form the basis for direction and control. Although there is a tendency towards oligarchy, there is also a consistent strain towards democracy in the functioning of groups. In its ability to control referral of matters to council committees, the group and the leaders can designate where and when various steps in the policy process will occur. In controlling the council agenda, the group can withdraw items, returning them to the committee for further work. They may also direct chairmen to make certain changes in committee recommendations. In practice, chairmen are expected to advise on modifications and to make judgements as to what the opposition will do and what the effect of change will be in the opinions of the officers.

However, service provision does not follow directly from party philosophy and group decision. There is usually an opposition party or parties ready with their own programmes and also ready to exploit the majority's difficulties. The majority is also concerned with community opinion, the need for services and the constraints on resources, particularly when it comes to setting the rates. The service to be provided and the nature of the issues also condition the actions of the party in control. Every service is unique in some aspect which will tend to blunt partisanship and doctrinaire approaches. Education, for example, deals with the lives and life chances of children, and within the service there is a strong tradition of professional educator control of curricular organization and classroom teaching. Thus there is a firm expectation that party politics must stop at the school door. Chapter 4 explores some of these matters and how they affect the policy process according to the perceptions of councillors, officers and others as they have reported them.

# 4 Constraints on the Policy Process

There are several constraints on the policy process which affect the decision-taking that is the process. Constraints impose conditions or limits on the policy-makers' actions to which they must respond. How they respond reflects the considerations that they believe must be made in the face of the constraints.

In local education authorities, it is councillors and officers who face the constraints and who respond. More accurately, it is the majority party working with education officers through the committee system who must decide which factors and forces will be taken into consideration. This means that some judgements about conditions and limitations are made from the point of view of party and the imperatives of party well-being. It also means that professional observations will be made. The two may not coincide but interact to create decision situations.

The various constraints identified by members and officers are those generally associated with the governance of English education at the local level. These include institutional arrangements and resource limitations such as central control and financing, local rates, coopted members of education committees and boards of school governors; there are the elements of uncertainty and risk as represented by public opinion and expectations as well as by more organized forces, interest groups of laymen and professional educators' associations. In each area, the perceptions of councillors and education officers are reported and, in places, the views of other local participants who interact with them in these areas.

## Central Control

Given an education system which is labelled as a national service locally administered, central government control as a constraint on local policy-making is of inevitable concern. How much of a constraint and in which particular respects can only be answered by those who make the policy and who operate the system in the local authority. When councillors were asked if education is controlled too much from the centre, nearly all felt that it was not. However, each councillor seemed to have his own perspective on the question and his own caveats to enter. The most pervasive point of view was that local authorities have sufficient autonomy to do what needs to be done in the way they feel it should be done. The chairman of one education committee, a Conservative, provided a typical answer, 'We implement national policies in the local education authority. Our actions and our policies alter the character of their policies to suit our needs and conditions. This is the freedom of the local education authority, indeed its responsibility.' The Labour leader in another authority said, 'We maintain the service—that is the big job and we are free in that respect. There is little interference or control.' The greatest difficulty was money; either there was not enough provided by the central government or there were too many tasks required of local government without due consideration of its financing problems. While no councillor wanted total central financing, many felt either that supplemental money should accompany mandates or that the local education authority should be permitted reasonable exceptions to national policy on the basis of ability to provide the funds. The responses imply that central government directives and financial stipulations present the local education authority with difficulties in arranging its priorities for policy-making.

These difficulties were borne out by those few councillors who felt that there is too much central control. Money was chiefly the root of their complaints. As one Conservative leader said, 'We are their servants on our money. We are asked to do too much by the central government. They forget we have many tasks as a government ourselves. Education isn't the only offender; all central departments do it.' The reorganization of secondary education was the prime example cited by these mainly Conservative and Independent members. Other educational problems had to be laid aside and had to be pushed down in priority, in order to begin going comprehensive. 'Now we're getting money for nursery education which we'd much prefer to have to complete reorganization', said an Independent leader.

Some councillors thought that the balance between central control and local freedom was about right. One perspective was that given by a Labour councillor speaking of the Conservative majority, 'If there were no central control, no centrally set standards, they'd not do half what they should do in education here.' Others saw the need to have national policies for distribution of resources, including teachers, and some reasonable assurance that there is adequate provision in all parts of the country. They were willing to accept the risk of blind enforcement and pressures towards uniformity. Consultation was seen by these councillors as a partial solution to this problem, and most felt that the opportunity of achieving reasonable compromises between the Department of Education and Science and local authorities already exists.

Officers were less divided on the question of central control because they view it from the perspectives of the authority and of their professional role. One chief executive felt that the central government demands too much spending by local authorities without guarantee of continued support. Changes in the rate support grant system in 1974, resulting in reduction of funds, were cited as an example. 'Both parties were very critical of this action,' he said, 'and I'd no real solutions to offer except to cut things we wanted to do locally. Good management practices go out of the window with that kind of pressure.' A chief education officer felt the same way, 'They irk me with pronouncements which cloak economizing as giving greater local freedom. It really puts more on the rates, which in this authority becomes a further limit on freedom.' Other views were tied to officers' interests in advancing the service. One chief education officer said, 'The local education authority has enormous opportunity to develop education for itself. The balance between central government and the local education authority is proper, because we here on the ground have real latitude to act.' There are choices to be made locally on the basis of local needs in some order of priority. The trick is to meet national aims while doing what the authority needs to do for itself and to avoid or minimize distortion of education provision by one or the other set of needs.

Yet, officers seem to dislike the task of finding professional rationales to prop up political decisions to go slow. As one chief education officer said, 'Straying localities have to be kept in line. Department of Education and Science helps the professional to do this by endorsing his interpretations of circulars and regulations to the council—if he's right.' Thus, while central financing practices complicate the officer's tasks, the knowledge that he can obtain bureaucratic backing for his professional stands is adequate compensation. It should be obvious, however, that officers do not use this backing as a threat. To do so would be to interfere in the professionals' primary objective of making the authority use its freedom and autonomy.

To test further the question of central control, councillors and officers were asked what they would do about a mandate from the central government to take some particular policy action. The most general answer from members was the following, 'We would obey the law.' Beyond that, nearly all councillors detailed political and other considerations to be made before complying. All the chief education officers said that they would interpret the mandate and would supply the committee with its meaning as it may apply to the local educational system. They agreed with members that the first decision was a political one to be made by the majority party. To sort out what is to be done and which tack is to be taken, the majority group asks itself two questions, as indicated by a Conservative education committee chairman, 'What stance will give the authority the best break by maximizing our benefits while retaining our freedom, and what leverage do we have for making our stance effective?' Leverage for making an effective stance may mean squeezing the Department of Education and Science for a necessary permission or aid in finding additional monies if there is rapid compliance. It also means finding the needed rationales to stave off pressure from the Department of Education and Science if going slow is the chosen alternative.

Another question is implied by the fact that the response is a political decision; this has to do with the match between local party aims and government policy. The lack of a match may result in a go-slow option. It seems to be of some importance who controls the government of the day and who is in the majority locally. Conservative leaders believe that they have a better chance to present their case and to receive dispensations if the Conservatives are the government. Labour leaders agreed, noting that a Labour government expects Labour councils to be first off the mark, but for both parties the decision to waffle has to take into account the make-up of the council. It becomes a calculated risk if either party has only a narrow majority. In the words of one Conservative leader, 'The socialists will use every opportunity to embarrass us, and there are Conservatives who feel much compelled to follow central government decrees.' Labour leaders do not fear defections but dislike being publicly labelled as law-breakers. 'We have the majority,' said one, 'but we are not irresponsible.'

The constraints imposed by central government control seem to be focused more on what they will mean within the authority than on what central government might do to the authority. The majority party seems far more concerned with local education authority freedom and reactions of the minority than with the Department of Education and Science. The law will be upheld ultimately, but it may be a long way round before the controlling party puts the pieces together the way it feels they should be in the light of local conditions. Officers feel that they have a different problem because they have to balance professional and community loyalties while observing political cues but that they must, at the same time, retain a professional stance. They use Department of Education and Science regulations when necessary to persuade the council but with some recognition of the limitations on such use imposed by the desirability of bringing the council majority to act out of enlightened community and self-interest.

## Resources and Rates

Education is the largest and most expensive service of the local authority. The size of the education establishment causes difficulties in its financing, almost as many difficulties as does the nature of the service. Compared with the other services it is, as one Department of Education and Science official noted, 'a whale among minnows'. About two-thirds to four-fifths of local expenditures are in the area of education. The service is labour-intensive, employing a large number of professionals who command higher salaries than do many other authority employees. The bulk of these are teachers whose numbers are determined largely by pupil enrolments, thus affording the authority little in the way of flexibility. Building and equipping schools is also costly, and again the numbers of pupils virtually dictate the need for facilities. This puts the service immediately up against the constraints of limited resources and the political question of the rates.

The first concern of every council is the rates. Many people judge how well or how poorly the council is doing by the rates it sets. The actual rate seems to be less important than the increases. As one councillor put it, during the 1974 rate revolt, 'People would gladly pay a penny in the pound rise but what they are protesting about is the monstrous 33% increase on top of a 15% increase last year.' The objective then is to keep the increases to a minimum. Education poses a twofold problem in this regard. First, in maintaining the service many costs are interrelated. More pupils means more teachers, more capitation, more transportation and other ancillary services. The rate grant support increases if enrolments are growing, but that is not enough. Some portion of these costs has to be borne by the rates. Second, there are 'start-up' and development costs for new activities and improvements. Personnel and their training and equipment and the renovation of spaces in schools all contribute to the mounting costs. With several projects underway at any one time, education costs escalate more quickly than those of other services. For the most part, these costs are reflected in the rates. Councillors have been told that change is essential to and synonymous with progress in a service such as education, but many are surprised at the price of change. Coupled with this are constant pressures to spend on education. Whether a central government directive, an innovation based on university research or a royal commission report or a need for a new local programme identified by the education department there is always something that must be done. The officers seem to be the single, most insistent source of pressure and always seem to have requests for additional funds under consideration. But as the chairman of one finance committee said, 'I would consider a chief education officer remiss in his work is he wasn't making such requests.'

What concerns councillors is not always the cost of education *per se* but the choices they have to make and the limited evidence on which to judge the results of expenditures. The enormity of the education budget rankles when it comes to making choices. 'Take a chairman whose service has a budget of £2,000,000,' said one policy and resources committee chairman. 'He sees us blithely add £100,000 to an education budget of £35,000,000, and all the time he's thinking what wonderful things his people could accomplish with just that added amount.' There is also the emotional tug of the children. As one member said, 'It is difficult to deny free milk to children because you feel you have to buy a new fire appliance.' The returns and benefits from spending are hard to see in the short term, both politically and socially. Councillors can point to a council housing project that accommodates a hundred families and can tell the electors that 'we did that'. There are few comparable results in education. There is also increasing criticism about how much the education service obtains for the pounds expended. Few specific replies were offered by councillors to illustrate this point, but several education committee chairmen said that their colleagues were requesting that some tightening up should take place in terms of 'doing more with what you've got by finding out what you do with what you get', to quote one Labour chairman. He went on to say, however, that most councillors have little understanding of management techniques such as programme analysis review or planning, programming, budgeting which would yield information in a systematic fashion. As that is the case, he cannot convince the council to finance the 'start-up' of one of these programmes.

When asked if the public felt that expenditures for education were too high, few councillors could cite objections from citizens. About the only items to which the public seems to react negatively are the buying of places in direct-grant schools and an occasional extra such as lighting a football pitch for night matches. (The first objection is not based solely on money.) No councillor could recall instances where education costs were criticized in the community as contributing to increases in the rates. Council housing or the redevelopment of a high street shopping precinct are more likely targets according to a Labour majority leader, 'and even some of the amenities we provide for old age pensioners such as footbridges over busy streets'. On the contrary, many councillors said that members of the public make frequent requests for greater educational expenditure.

Chief education officers see the financial constraints from a different perspective. Generally, they agreed that there is never enough money for what they believe should be done, reflecting a condition endemic to the profession. More realistically, they felt that their councils supported education. One chief education officer in a county authority, faced with the special burdens of local government reorganization, mounting inflation and central government reductions in rate support, could still say, 'Progress? No, but the council has supported this service and has kept it effective.' The greatest problem that officers say exists are the ceilings on rate increases or budgets imposed by policy and resources or finance committees. Most chief officers think that they have a better chance of obtaining the kind of funds they need if they can compete and if they can have an opportunity to provide rationales and to demonstrate their cases. If there are ceilings, it is new developments that are usually cut or that are given lower priority by the education committee. Some policy and resources committees are very tough about setting limits, even to the extent of forgetting political proprieties. In one authority, the chairman of the education committee apparently was not vigorous enough about impressing budget reductions on the committee. The chief education officer was called in by the policy committee and was told to achieve this. 'The chief was visibly angered by both the mandate and the method,' said one of his associates, 'but he never said a word about it.' The reductions were made through his revised recommendations. (The chairman was replaced by his party group a few months later.) Officers understand the political reasoning that can lead to the setting of ceilings; indeed, they like to know the broad boundaries within which to set their own expectations. However, as they have to justify their requests, they feel that artificial ceilings, imposed without explanation, tend to yield distorted pictures of service needs.

Education policy must be considered in the light of costs and their impact on the rates. However, the most important limiting factor is not the actual spending plans but the majority's perception of the political impact of rate increases. How much of this political impact can be attributed to education is apparently hard to judge in the absence of citizens' complaints linking education costs to rate rises. Therefore, the majority is forced back on its own judgements and evaluations of councillors' views of the question. Education is a large service and thus a large target. Its non-tangible benefits and delayed benefits add to the temptation to whittle away its funds. The mandatory nature of much educational expenditure means that items not going towards basic provision are likely to be cut. It is precisely these developmental and added service areas that officers see as fulfilling identified needs and as contributing to educational progress. As professionals they dislike the artificiality of ceilings but realize that ceilings represent the majority's view of political reality.

## Structure

Two structural elements within the education scheme require consideration as constraints on the policy-making process. These are coopted members of the education committee and boards of governors. While both are usually well controlled through the application of party political screening to the appointment process, it seems that coopted members and governors are of concern to councillors and officers as they make process decisions. For the most part, this concern centres on the potentials of coopted members and governors for embarrassing the majority either through mistakes or through token resistance. Additionally, heads of schools may combine with governors, giving a professional push to the resistance. This means that the majority may have to apply pressure or to take up the matter at another time and place purely on party lines, moves which in themselves may be embarrassing. This may not be the sole reason, however.

### Coopted Members

As noted earlier, the cooptation of persons interested and experienced in education onto the education committee is required by the Education Act of 1944. The usual memberships are three churchmen, Anglican, Roman Catholic and Free Church, and teacher representatives, allocated in proportion to their local memberships, to the National Union of Teachers, the National Association of Schoolmasters and the Joint Four. Others evincing general knowledge of and interest in education are appointed, perhaps as individuals or from home-school associations, trade unions or community groups. All are appointed through the education committee which means that each candidate is subject to the majority party's approval. There is very seldom a hard political scrutiny of the clergy, although the Conservatives in some places accuse Labour of leaning towards 'red priests'. The teachers' unions are usually left to their own devices to fill their allotted seats. Occasionally, when the unions do not act jointly in doing so, Labour will object if there seems to be an excess of candidates from the National Association of Schoolmasters, feeling that they lean towards the Conservatives' view on education. However, both parties complain that the teachers often select 'the hacks and time-servers of union politics' for coopted seats. It is in the appointment of other coopted members that the parties in council screen carefully for political outlook through councillors' nominations, education committee's recommendations and group decisions.

Party control of coopted members is quite heavy handed and clumsy. In the three Outer London boroughs, almost complete party control prevails. General coopted places are allotted to each party in accordance with its proportional strength in council. Many of those appointed are, to sum up officers' opinions, 'defeated council candidates, ward organization people, former councillors or their wives and leaders of organizations whose political sympathies are well known'. Councillors tended to agree, especially when speaking of the other party's appointees. In the three counties, the number of coopted members shrunk as the committee size was reduced at reorganization, and the remaining places came under tight majority control. Teachers' representatives often took the brunt of the reduction, and in one county they lost 6 places out of 9. The move is towards ensuring a preponderant number of committee seats for the elected members of the majority party. Coopted members were not always politically screened before, but they are now. The reference point is the majority leader who can obtain advice on candidates from his group or who can take it on himself to approve the selections as sent up by the education committee. To one Conservative minority leader, this is a retrograde step, 'Ten years ago coopted members were political pawns here. I put a stop to it as chairman of education. Now Labour is doing just what my party did before I came in.' The results so far have been an increasing number of former councillors and other friends of the controlling party filling most coopted seats in these counties. There is a partial exception in one, however. Subcommittees make their own cooptations for subcommittee service only, and the chief education officer feels that these people are relatively untainted. However, the participation of coopted members in all six authorities is surrounded by such conventions as the following: they may not serve on subcommittees; if they do, they may not vote; and if they can vote in subcommittees, they may not have a vote on the main committee; then, if they do and the chairman deems an item a party matter, coopted members must abstain from voting. Many times they cannot obtain the information which most majority elected members can. Officers complain about this but withhold information, on the advice of their chairmen, until the time of the meeting.

Given the high degree of political control over the appointments and actions of coopted members, it is difficult to perceive the factors that would make them constraints in policy-making. There seem to be two points inferred by councillors and officers. First, coopted teachers and clergymen are informed people about schools and the community. They have potential as articulate communicators between the people they represent and the committee. 'They take ideas away for discussion,' said one Labour chairman, 'so, when they speak up at the next meeting, we listen.' Second, coopted members seem to represent constituencies, some well-organized like teachers' unions, others not so well-organized like home–school associations. Councillors are wary that these potentials can become pressure points. 'They take the side of the have-nots; they press us to provide more money. They can get it in subcommittees, and sometimes it's difficult to knock it all out in the main committee,' said one Conservative leader. However, both councillors and officers agree that there is a high degree of variability in the quality and contributions of all appointees. Many of the appointees are confused too. 'Who do I represent?' said a home–school federation secretary, 'some nights the federation, other nights the general public, sometimes me. I'm quitting soon because it's all too political now—to get things done I have to make alliances with people I don't particularly like.' The influence of coopted members may best be summed up by the view of several chief education officers. When active and interested, they are a somewhat stablizing force because of their special interest knowledge, and, when this is combined with their nominal representational roles, it helps to keep party excesses to a minimum; however, when made up of party and union hacks, coopted members are a relatively meaningless bit of window dressing.

## School Governors

Each state school, or group of schools, has a board of governors or managers appointed under the instruments of government drawn up by the local authority. Essentially this means that each school is separate from the authority in so far as the duties of the governors are specified. The usual statements, adapted from the Model Articles of Government in the Education Act of 1944, place responsibility for the conduct and curriculum of the school on the board. The head, in consultation with the governors, is responsible for the internal organization, management and discipline of the school. Thus the authority determines the general educational character of the school within the local system and supervises its staffing and financing, but each school is to 'have a life of its own'.

This separation is more apparent than real in so far as policy-making is concerned in politically controlled authorities. As with coopted members of the education committee, school governors are appointed with the approval of the majority party. This is particularly true in the London boroughs that were studied where many councillors sit on governing bodies. The ratio by parties is usually two to one for the majority, although three to one is not unknown. If there is a seat for a parent, he or she can be expected to be either sympathetic to the majority or neutral. Heads or teachers may also get to fill a place, but it is not clear what orthodoxies are expected. There is less information about governors' appointments in the counties. All three chief education officers felt that the governing system needed overhaul, noting that there were many vacancies and that some governing boards had not met in years. However, political control of governors' appointments is taking over. In one county, party leaders have decided that boards will reflect the political make-up of the council, and many governors have already been named. The chief education officer was obviously disappointed, 'I had hoped that district councils and the electors in each school area would have some say.' In another county, the Independent-Conservative majority is expected to move to control appointments, since they found out that Labour has been carefully selecting and promoting its people through what has been considered an open system.

Judging from interviews in the Outer London boroughs, councillors appointed as school governors see their role as one of getting authority policies carried out in the schools. When asked who they represent, most said either the education committee or the council. A few felt that they represented their party. While none said that they represented the public or the school, several believed that they had a duty to defend the school from authority policies which 'get too specific and seem to threaten the school's independence', as one minority party councillor said. However, as pipelines into the political system, governors seem to have a limited usefulness. Heads thought that governors were useful in obtaining extra equipment and some minor repairs and in getting street cross-walks designated but that they could not become the centres for advocating policy modification or change. Parent governors in two authorities were critical of the party appointees in just this respect, and, as one said, 'If they see an advantage to one or both parties in doing some little thing, then they do it.' The view was that the politicians stay together, effectively overriding the desires of parent and other governing body members. 'We worked for three years to get parent places on governing boards,' said one interest group leader, 'but, when we did, we found the politicians in control there too. It was very disappointing.'

Education officers were almost equally sanguine. Most believe that governors are now a party political problem. Occasionally, a head will get his board to press hard for an exception to a policy, but after an officer explains the consequences to the committee it is then left to the majority party to get the governors back into line. However, there is a certain sensitivity because councillor–governors can become focal points for discontent within the party group if small problems go unattended. If cases build up without being reported to officers by the committee chairman, there is danger. Therefore, officers monitor governors' meetings and keep on the look-out for matters raised by governors as a kind of early warning network.

## Heads of Schools

The usual view of heads as constraints on policy-making is that they can become an obstructionist element within the structure. This is most often seen at the point where local education authority policy as interpreted by the officers appears to conflict with the freedom of the head to work out how his school will set about achieving objectives set by the authority. In such situations, heads often turn to their governors for help in varying the timetable of change or the added resources needed to meet expectations set. It is done rather adroitly by developing rationales, by making an occasional telephone call and by playing on the predilection of politicians to make promises. The result is a mild pressure on the chief education officer to look into making some adjustments.

For the most part, however, heads avoid hard politics in the policy process. There appear to be two reasons behind their attitude. First, it does not seem to be compatible with the professional aura they want to maintain. Being known as professionals lends credence to the requests they make of politicians. Acting professionally affords a better basis for consultation with officers. If a head becomes involved in the politics of issues, his colleagues feel he is doing them all a disfavour by bringing politics closer to all the schools. Second, heads, particularly in urban areas, appear to want more direction and guidance from the local education authority as problems become more complex. 'Take immigrants,' said one head. 'There is experience around and the borough has time to prepare. If solutions are left to each head, we'll make a muddle of it.' He went on to say that the officers should make analyses and should obtain the most useful policies they can for a borough-wide approach. Obviously, heads playing politics would interfere with the officers' roles in obtaining useful policies in the education committee. Heads still want to be consulted but increasingly find that they have insufficient knowledge about authority finances or conditions in other parts of the system generally to contribute to solving problems.

Education officers are not so sure that heads take pains to avoid being political. 'They fly kites to test the breezes around election time,' said one deputy, 'and they hold back on suggestions until they see which way the new council is going to go on education.' Heads have been known to air their complaints in the newspapers if they feel that the governors and the authority have not acted on such matters as requested building repairs. On major questions, chief education officers can ultimately make the controlling party take away the support a head is receiving from his governors. 'Then he's my problem', said one chief education officer, 'and we can usually work it all out, once he understands that the political gambit is over.'

Coopted members and school governors are not very important as constraints on policy-making. The political system has expanded to control them through the usual organizing methods of political parties when in government. Mere organizing may not be sufficient, however. Occasionally, the nature of the appointees or the situation of the school versus the authority may lead them to act differently from expected. In the latter instances, heads may be providing impetus and information. Thus, while officers tend to think of coopted members and governors as politicians' problems, they do watch them carefully. The final responsibility for their actions rests with the parties that appointed them. Heads, once separated from political support, can be dealt with on a professional basis.

## The Public

The public provides a set of constraints on the policy process which are reflected in the kinds of decisions that have to be made. For the most part, officers and members say that citizens are concerned only about the school their children attend or the school in the neighbourhood or village. If everything is all right there, then everything is all right everywhere—or almost all right. The best estimates are that each school has its few dozen active supporters, usually parents who see that the extra curricula fund-raising is done and who can be expected to speak to their councillor about the need for painting the woodwork or for seeding the lawn if the head thinks it necessary. There are also one or two detractors for each school, people who find fault, who send letters to the newspapers and who complain to governors or councillors. Apart from that, councillors say they hear little from the schools unless the head or a teacher mishandles some incident.

Councillors and officers identified three other areas of latent public concern that impinge on educational policy-making by the authority. First, there are neighbourhood or sectional rivalries over who is getting (or not getting) what from the council. Second, there is the siting of schools or other educational facilities. Third, there is a legacy of discontent from the struggles over the reorganization of secondary education such as the taking of places in direct-grant schools, the allocation of pupils to maintained secondary schools and the possibility of the last stands to be made over the last schools to go comprehensive. In all six authorities studied, no party leader, whether of the majority or minority party, believed that public dissatisfaction in any of these three areas could lead to the defeat of the controlling party. However, there is the potential for disruptive quarrels, leading to erosion of political support so that the parties, particularly the majority party, have to keep alert as they make policy.

## Sectionalism

Sectional rivalries appear in several different ways. Local government reorganization contributed a great deal to the problem in five of the six authorities. In two counties, it is an incipient battle between rural areas and the boroughs over who is getting their schools upgraded and who is not. In the third, there is resentment over the resources being poured into a new town. The Outer London boroughs divide somewhat on former town lines, but more emphasis is now being placed on social class distinctions between sections of each community. On this point, each party accuses the other of inflaming the rivalry with campaign oratory and council debates. In one of these authorities, there is a growing immigrant population which is becoming the object of complaints as the council makes efforts to alleviate the severe problems in that section of the borough.

Councillors seem to react to these rivalries in three different ways. The most usual reaction is that the council cannot win no matter what it does. 'I've shown my people charts and I've compared expenditures school by school,' said one Conservative councillor, 'and they still won't believe that we are giving them as much as the south of the borough just because our party doesn't control the council; but they had the same complaint when we did.' A Labour leader said that his party used to try to do something in each section of the borough, '. . . a new school there this year, a playground here next year, but someone always wanted to jump the queue. Now we go strictly on need as the officers request. That leaves it to me to put down the rebellions.' The second type of reaction is that of trying to keep discontent at a minimum and to avoid public outcry. Thus, the squeaking wheel gets oiled despite other needs. 'Some people won't ask anything of us; others want more and more. All it takes is one member who wants to make a name for himself and we're into it,' said one education committee chairman. He went on to say, 'It is the group's fault because if a councillor wants something for his section he can usually get it.' This type of reaction in one of the counties is causing the Labour-controlled authority to have four sets of policy, in essence, for education; one for each of the two boroughs absorbed at reorganization, one for the rural schools and one set of new county-wide policies fitted around the other sets. 'It is not politically feasible to take away something a borough has had, and it is not financially feasible to treat the outlying schools to the benefits enjoyed by the boroughs,' said the chairman. The minority leader felt that his people found it easy to blame Labour for the problem, forgetting that when they controlled the old council they had let some village schools deteriorate because their people did not complain. The third reaction of councillors is to mark off sectionalism as pure politics. The existing divisions in the community are used as vehicles for one party to strike out at the other. One chief education officer made this observation, 'Education is a topic in which people are interested. It is not a vote winner for politicians, not yet; but more and more it is tied to party political views and parties take stands on the issues. That makes the tie.' The next step is easy. 'Take a Section 13 notice to change the character of a school,' said a Conservative councillor, 'The first question is about the educational consequences, but it becomes political when you move to get it done.' Such an item could remain a political question (with a small 'p'); the sorting out of views between people if party ideologies did not intrude, according to a number of councillors. However, one party tells people that the other party is taking away their school or, conversely, is trying to prevent this improvement in education for their children. 'Parties seize too quickly on local concerns,' said one Labour leader, 'but we have our party views on education. Given the complexity of education, there are few aspects that do not touch us somewhere, and we are responsible to those who elected us.'

## School Sites

The siting of schools is another concern which councillors are wary of in making policy. Oddly enough, while people want many things from the government, no one seems to want a schoolhouse at the foot of his garden. One Labour chairman gave an example, 'We needed to build an educationally subnormal facility. We got complaints from the locality we chose. A few Conservatives have tried to ride it as a political issue, but in the end I'm sure both parties will endorse the proposal. Sites can't become political footballs or we'll never get our schools built.' The chief education officer in a county authority noted that people do not want the school too near but that they do not want it too far away either; therefore, much time is devoted to site selection. A related problem is the use of compulsory purchase orders to obtain land for educational purposes. People do not like to have the price settled by fiat, regardless of the safeguards on fairness. Many Conservative and Independent councillors dislike compulsory purchase as a matter of principle but feel that the council pays too much when it negotiates a price. Labour-controlled councils use compulsory purchase readily but have found it increasingly unpopular. The Labour vice-chairman of education and the housing committee chairman lost their council seats, while the party retained control in one London borough. The Conservative campaign in their admittedly marginal ward focused on the compulsory purchase order issue and apparently tipped the balance.

## Going Comprehensive

All six authorities studied have been largely reorganized along comprehensive lines. The few schools that remain to be decided about will cause some difficulty, but the struggles in the council will be over timing and methods, not the basic principle. Each faces a different set of problems, however. In the counties, chief education officers noted that secondary reorganization stopped when local government reorganization began. 'I have to get them moving again,' said one chief education officer, 'and I don't relish the thought.' His particular problem was explained by the chief executive, 'Comprehensives came early but not enthusiastically to this county. The landed interests combined with the few Labourites in a classic seventeenth-century way to defeat the rising middle class. With reorganization the gentry left the council, and that same middle class is now in control.' In another county, Labour has come to power for the first time in a dozen years with the toughest problems in going comprehensive still remaining unresolved. Curiously enough, the decisions they have to make concern some grammar schools in former county boroughs long controlled by Labour. In the third county, a deputy education officer said, 'The pro- and anti-factions are out there, slumbering until we make a move. I'm sure the council will move. Like all counties we are now more closely divided, and Labour is going to prod the majority effectively on this.'

In the Outer London boroughs, there are more difficulties with the consequences of previous actions than with changing the character of remaining grammar schools. Paired schools, split sites, competition for the shrinking number of grammar school places, impending cut-offs in taking direct-grant school places and ending the eleven-plus examination are more important issues to the public. Each year there is the matter of allocation of pupils to secondary schools, and each year there are problems. 'Sometimes I don't think we'll ever get it right,' said one Labour member, 'I'm almost glad we are the minority when the complaints come in.' Some members feel that it does not concern them, that the education committee made the situation and that they should bear the responsibility. One Conservative chairman said he would not let his group get away with that, 'They are going to come to the group tonight with all the parents' complaints from last week's allocation announcement. They are going to have a go at me, but I'll remind them that they approved the policy, knowing that the chief education officer said it would bring complaints from about 10% of the parents.'

The stopping of direct-grant places as part of going comprehensive is particularly hard for Conservative councillors but as one said, 'The officers have convinced us on this one and we'll stand by it.' In one authority, a complete foreclosure has been instituted by Labour which still brings a few un-complimentary remarks from Conservatives at opportune moments in debates on other educational issues. It will be very similar for the eventual elimination of the eleven-plus examinations. Officers and the teaching profession will convince elected members that this vestigial remain cannot be justified on educational grounds. Now that the big prizes of selection have been eliminated, councillors will be left with the task of soothing away the emotional sting of ending the eleven-plus. As one Conservative said, 'The main battle is over. We now have the problem of helping our people to live with the changes in schooling, knowing full well what their sensitivities are.'

Constraints imposed on the policy process for education by the public seem to arise mainly from the fact that councillors listen to the public through local party earphones. The key is in the one leader's phrase ' . . . *we are responsible to those who elected us'*. *Those* refers to party supporters and not to the general public. Certainly there are issues and matters of concern, but these are vehicles which provide challenges to the party to keep its word. This may mean giving demonstrable benefits to sections of the community where party support exists, easing the pain of going comprehensive (for the Conservatives) or speedily completing secondary reorganization (for Labour). However, the controlling party also has to pay attenton to community-wide needs or to service provision to demonstrate responsibility. Therefore, it may avoid politics in siting schools, or it may completely override the political aspects of sectionalism. As a majority, it is always constrained to avoid the excesses of party, simply because the minority party can never really be labelled with committing partisan excesses.

Although the focus of this section has been on councillors' perceptions of the public, the meaning of these constraints for education officers should be clear. Education is not a vote winner for politicians, but it is obvious that politicians see education in relation to certain circumstances which can lead to the erosion of their support if it is not handled properly. Thus, education officers would seem to be equally constrained by the majority party's beliefs as to where its support is in the community.

## Interest Groups

In the opinion of officers and councillors there are two types of local interest groups which act as constraints on the policy process for education. One is the organizations of lay people concerned with schools and educational provision, indigenous to the community but perhaps with affiliation to a national association or federation with similar purposes. The other type is the professional associations and the unions of educators in local schools. They, of course, have close organizational ties to their national groups, and on general employment objectives they follow the national leadership. At the local level, their concerns are twofold: the improvement of working conditions in schools and the professional role in improving education. For both types of groups it is difficult to separate national organization influences from local association objectives and action programmes. No systematic attempt will be made to do so. Instead, the national influences as stressed by the groups themselves or by councillors and officers will be used.

## Lay Organizations

One of the first things which has to be noted is that officers and councillors make a careful distinction between school parents' groups or neighbourhood school associations and interest groups. An association which is clearly identified with a particular school, confines its activities to promoting the welfare of that school and avoids involvement in other places is not classified as an interest group. Their treatment is different, too. Officials go to considerable lengths to get acquainted with school associations, to speak at their meetings if invited and otherwise to maintain goodwill. Interest groups, on the other hand, are received with civility, but closeness is avoided, particularly by officers. An officer consorting with or captured by an interest group becomes *persona non grata* with elected members. Yet, school associations are watched almost as closely as interest groups. As one councillor said (and a number of headmasters testified), 'You can never tell when they will turn on you.'

It was surprising to find that there are so few lay organizations which local officials readily identify as interest groups actively supporting or promoting aspects of education and seeking policy changes. County councillors and officers mentioned only scattered local units of the better-known national organizations such as the Confederation for the Advancement of State Education which is pro-comprehensive, pro-state expansion and financing, the National Education Association which is pro-grammar school, pro-parents' rights and pro-high standards. There were also a few parent-teacher federations active in seeking council action, but their ties to the National Confederation of Parent-Teacher Associations were, as might be expected, quite non-existent. 'We hear from school associations occasionally and from individuals, but large organized efforts don't happen,' said one chief education officer. A Labour member in another county said, 'We don't have interest groups as such to deal with. It's all individual complaints or requests.' There was some feeling in the third county that its several interest groups were dormant and were likely to stay that way until further secondary reorganization proposals are introduced. The question hinges on the proposals that are made and the groups that exist in the newly annexed boroughs and whether or not these groups combine with the weak county groups. The Outer London boroughs present a somewhat different scene. While there were still few interest groups that could be identified, those that do exist are considered active and potentially troublesome. Most frequently mentioned again² were the better-known national organizations with local units. There was no evidence of alliances or coalitions of these groups within any community, although in one authority several *ad hoc* combinations were generally known to exist during past crises. Much of what follows is based on results in the London boroughs and may not apply to the counties.

Local educational interest groups are not well thought of by councillors. They are considered too strident in the presentation of their cases, are poorly informed as to what the authority is actually doing and have not usually sought relief through appropriate channels such as the governors and the officers. Stridency includes writing letters to local newspapers (which are, incidentally, interested in and devote much space to education groups), bringing inflammatory outsiders to speak at meetings and descending *en masse* on education committee sessions. For their information, councillors feel that interest groups read or hear about the problems of schools in other places through the efforts of their national affiliates and that they immediately apply those to local schools without further investigation. While some matters are taken up with officers as a means of seeking relief, governors are not contacted. 'If they were asked, the governors could answer most questions,' said one councillor, 'The education committee shouldn't have to be bothered with unsubstantiated claims.'

Interest group leaders have an entirely different viewpoint. Publicity is a first essential, because officials keep school difficulties to themselves. Many activities such as newspaper stories, speakers and petitioning are undertaken to attract the attention of the public as well as the council. 'It is so difficult,' complained one organization secretary, 'People here are concerned only with their own school, if that. We can't get people stirred up about problems in the authority.' As to the information supplied by national affiliates, most leaders said that it only provides starting points for local investigation. However, the availability of information about local situations is almost nil, and local groups do not have the capacity, personnel and money to examine educational questions extensively. Interest group leaders are extremely unhappy about the pressure they have to bring to bear on heads and officers in order to obtain the required facts and figures. They are convinced that the withholding of information is often deliberate. Those organizations which have coopted seats on the education committee feel that they are given somewhat more information but that they do not really have greater access to information. Finally, in seeking relief, interest groups claim that they do start with governors and officers, but need to move on to the committee and council when they find it is necessary to be heard at the upper levels of the hierarchy. Most interest groups are federated and organized in school or neighbourhood units, while those few that are authority-wide proceed on the basis of requests for action in one or more schools; thus the school is a natural starting point. Regardless, organization leaders have found by experience that governors are useless bodies for achieving anything. Officers, on the other hand, are deemed to be important contacts. If the interest group's point of view has not been precluded by officers' understandings of the majority's point of view, then such contact may be the first real step towards consideration. Obviously, if party views seem likely to prevail, it is councillors who must be reached.

Given the jaundiced view of interest groups held by elected members, how do they perceive them as constraints on the policy-making process? The first point is that interest groups are more or less organized and fairly knowledgeable about the workings of educational government, if not politics. As they are organized, they can achieve something. For example, in one authority, lay interest groups alone were instrumental in delaying two schools going comprehensive; this was achieved by organizing letter-writing campaigns through which the Secretary of State was presented with a torrent of objections to the scheme, following publication of a Section 13 notice. The second point is the ability to publicize and to create some semblance of public discontent over a matter. The target is the majority party group, and the purpose is to upset their timing, bringing about a more partisan stand earlier in the process. Hopefully this has a ripple effect, and people not provoked by the educational question may be stimulated by an overt party political action. For example, as part of a long-range programme to improve facilities, one Conservative-controlled authority planned to close old small schools and to consolidate catchment areas while seeking to build new larger facilities. One of the first closures was scheduled for a working-class area. Several interest groups objected, pointing out that it was not the children of Conservative members and their friends who would have to travel out of their neigh-- bourhood to school. The Conservative majority kept to the programme timetable but without Labour or Liberal votes, according to one member, 'leaving people with another example of Tory arrogance'.

As might be suspected from these examples, some interest groups are ideologically aligned with one or the other political party. This is often clear from an organization's stated objectives and perhaps is recognized in its being coopted. Often there are governors, councillors and teachers of known political leanings on the membership rolls of the organization. While there were no strong indications that local interest groups were fronts for the parties or that councillors were captives, the question arises whether the political friendship of interest groups is a constraint on policy-making. The answer seems to be that party responsibility is divisible from organizational friendships, making other considerations more important. By way of illustration from one authority, the leader of an organization, friendly to the majority party , said, 'We know what is going on politically, and we know when we can have an effect and when we can't.' She cited a current controversy involving two schools and indicated that the majority had made up its mind about a solution only with great difficulty. The organization did not like the solution on ideological grounds but reluctantly withheld its public opposition. 'The majority knew how we felt and they didn't care,' said the leader. Another interest group, friendly to the other party, also stayed out of the controversy. When it was asked why it had done so when it was obvious that the minority wanted to capitalize on the majority's difficulty, their secretary said, 'Our people in that school area asked us not to enter the controversy', implying that the organization was more responsive to its constituent units than to an ideological alignment.

The next section deals with the second type of interest group, teachers' organizations.

### Teachers' Organizations

From the perspective of the local authority, organized teacher pressure or resistance can effectively disrupt the development of policy and its planned implementation. From the teachers' perspective, teacher welfare and working conditions are affected by authority policies. They also have an interest in contributing to policy development, stemming from the professionals' concern for influencing the directions that are being taken in their field. Both local officials and teachers' leaders realize that teachers' professional advice and skills as well as their physical presence are necessary to operate the educational system. In times of stress, teachers' demonstrated goodwill is essential to prevent divisions which opposition parties and other interest groups might exploit in making issues controversial.

A number of more important considerations do not enter the picture. General conditions of teacher employment are set nationally, and basic salary scales are decided through Burnham Committee negotiations in which the major unions, the local government associations and the Department of Education and Science participate. In addition, there are local understandings made with teacher unions and associations in the light of nationally agreed items. With these out of the way for the most part, both officials and teachers can focus attention on ongoing activities and on what they mean for the relationships between the two and the shaping of the educational system at the operating end.

As a result, teachers' organizations receive completely different consideration from other interest groups. Five of the six authorities studied had, in addition to coopted places for teachers, one or more consultative bodies through which council members and/or officers meet with teachers' representatives. While parties monitor the appointments of governors and coopted members, teachers are usually left to their own devices to fill seats on consultative bodies. Often the only stipulation is that the different school levels, primary, secondary and special, etc., are represented. Apart from this, different unions and associations seem to operate quite freely, sorting out their own politics and electing or appointing their people who will meet regularly with local officials.

There may be as many as nine unions and professional associations active among the teachers of an authority. The major ones are the National Union of Teachers which is composed largely of primary teachers but usually with a sufficient number of secondary teachers to claim that they represent the full range of education, the National Association of Schoolmasters which is an all-male organization composed mostly of secondary teachers, and the Joint Four which is a confederation of the Associations of Head Masters, Head Mistresses, Assistant Masters and Assistant Mistresses. Each of these organizations has certain professional and political proclivities attributed to it at the national level which are well reflected in local units. For example, the National Union of Teachers is concerned with continued progress on secondary reorganization, is considered sympathetic towards Labour and prefers to pursue its objectives quietly within education's officialdom. The National Association of Schoolmasters is regarded as more militant, dedicated to what it defines as the career teacher, very concerned with preserving academic standards and teachers' prerogatives while improving the education system. The Joint Four is considered to be the old guard protecting the grammar school, the ties with independent schools and the privileges of heads. Other associations, some splinters and satellites of the major organizations and some groups of specialized teachers, exist in local authorities but because of small numbers do not usually achieve separate representation.

Five of the authorities have some federated form of organization designated by the authority as an agency through which teachers are represented. It may be called the teachers' council, the consultative committee or the advisory group. Two authorities stipulate that representation is by school level, including special teachers; two authorities strike a balance with about half the teachers' panel elected by level and half appointed by their unions. The fifth uses union representation only. In the sixth authority, there is a teachers' council on paper, but it has not been active since 1965, and each union or school staff is free to schedule meetings with the education committee to take up their questions, according to the chairman. The teachers' organizations would like to have only union and association representation. This has virtually been achieved now, as elections by school level usually go in favour of organization candidates. In one authority dominated by a National Union of Teachers membership, this is recognized and, therefore, several places are filled by the authority with National Association of Schoolmasters and Joint Four teachers selected, of course, from appropriate school levels.

The teachers' panel usually meets with a panel of education committee members, similarly to a subcommittee. In one county, the members' panel is made up of subcommittee chairmen, and in another it is the coordinating subcommittee. Normally each panel may submit items for the agenda. Votes are not taken, but minutes are kept and include recommendations to the education committee. The frequency of meeting varies from once a cycle to twice a year. Where meetings are infrequent, the teachers' panel also meets with the officers two or three times a year.

The functions of these consultative arrangements are difficult to define because they range over many topics in different ways. Most generally, it is an information exchange in which the authority tells teachers what it is doing, and teachers give their reactions. At the same time, teachers have the opportunity to question members about the past and future actions. Naturally, the teachers' point of view is the effects on the working conditions, the professional prerogatives and the professional role in carrying out decisions. The National Union of Teachers and the Joint Four leaders feel that such meetings help to detail the professionals' contributions within both general national agreements and local understandings. As one said, 'This is where we spell out many things, from which amenities will be included in staff lounges to corporal punishment and on to the educational effects of going comprehensive.' The authority retains the initiative, however. Proposals are tested, not as alternatives but as items under development, and teachers can enter their caveats for authority consideration. Officials usually keep negotiation out of the picture. 'That question is for another time and place', said one chairman responding to an objection to Saturday games supervision at a joint meeting. This brought a muttered comment from the representative of the National Association of Schoolmasters that the joint advisory was '. . . nothing but a talking shop', a usual criticism. However, as another chairman noted, 'Each union gets its own chance because, by policy, each is solicited for its specific reactions to policies we plan to announce. What we want in the consultative committee is the professional response.'

Much of this area of endeavour remains murky. Leaders of the teachers' organizations find the arrangements suitable as an avenue for being heard by the majority and for being in on some decisions. While the National Association of Schoolmasters often says these bodies are 'cumbersome and claptrap', even they agree that there are some tangible benefits for the profession and the schools. Councillors, as might be expected, praise the results as keeping up good relations with teachers, keeping controversy out and generally giving the authority a good image as being responsive to teachers as professionals. Officers are not as convinced on any of these scores. Many think it is more important to involve teachers in specific activities such as planning, curriculum development and community projects, letting questions and participation arise naturally. They dislike organization leaders directing teachers' opinions. To sum it up, officers report that the distance between teachers and administrators as fellow professionals is growing, because teachers are courted by politicians. Informal contacts between officers and teachers seem fewer and less important. Union and association leaders sometimes prefer and promote their objectives directly with party leaders, bypassing officers and even education committee chairmen.

Teachers' organizations are recognized as constraining forces in educational policy-making. As interest groups for professional educators, they are deeply embedded in each authority's educational operation. Coping with them is a problem for local officials and this is done through provision of some common meeting grounds, consultative bodies. However, there is an uneasiness about these arrangements on the part of councillors and officers

that stems from a combination of the limited control they have
through them and the increasing desires of some organizations
for greater say in policy matters.

## Summary

Several constraints on policy-making for education were
examined. Central control, resources and rates, coopted members
and governors, the public and interest groups each contribute to
the considerations which councillors and officers have to make in
reaching process decisions. In part, constraints arise because of
the manner in which these factors and forces are related to
education. Central control means that the law must ultimately be
obeyed, although local processes can be used to delay and bend
directives for local benefit. The structural elements that provide
for broader participation have been reduced as uncertainties
through extending party influences into the appointment process
for coopted members and governors; yet, this is no guarantee of
conformity. The cooperation of organized teachers needs to be
solicited, because their services are vital to the operation of the
system. Constraints also arise from councillors' perceptions, as
they look and listen through the filters of party interests and the
imperatives of party control. Resource allocation has a bearing on
the question of rate increases, a point which politicians feel they
can ignore only at great peril. Matters that concern the public, as
expressed in sectionalism, the siting of schools and secondary
reorganization issues are seen first from the point of view of their
contribution to the erosion of party support and then as educational problems to be solved. Interest groups are seen as noisy,
possibly troublesome organizations but groups that need
watching precisely because they are organized.

Education officers recognize the same constraints but not
always from the same perspectives. The professional concern,
they have provides somewhat different views, usually along the
line of getting what they need to do the job, e.g. bureaucratic
backing from the Department of Education and Science, a fair
share of resource allocation and a full hearing for their expert
opinions. While they need to understand the politician's concern,
they cannot totally substitute it for their own views as officers. At
the same time, however, getting the job done in the local

education authority means accommodating the constraints as seen by elected members.

In the next chapter, the key participants in the policy process will be examined, and their complementary roles will be described.

# 5 Participants in the Process

The main participants in the policy process carry out complex roles within the local government. Their roles and interrelationships have a bearing on the process decisions which are made in the development and choice of policies for education. This chapter will examine the roles and interrelationships from the viewpoint of the participants.

The policy subsystem for education consists of the education department, the education committee and subcommittees, the majority party group and the council. While not mutually exclusive, the generalized roles of each can be identified as follows: the department and the committee initiate and develop policy proposals, while the group and the council decide or ratify policy choices. The main participants in the policy process are the officers and elected members who organize and direct the activities of each part of the subsystem. Within the department it is the chief education officer, and in the committee it is the chairman. The main participant in the party group and in the council is the majority leader. In terms of the policy process, the leader's role in the policy and resources committee may be readily susbstituted for his role in the council. The roles they carry out are based on the generalized roles but are not limited to them, particularly when it comes to conducting the relationships between parts of the subsystem.

The most critical aspects of the main participants' roles are those which link them together in the policy process such as making recommendations, giving advice or directions and exerting influence. These relationships are shown in Figure 1. When policy questions arise, the responses are proposed to the education committee by the chief education officer. He also

Figure 1: The Policy System for Education

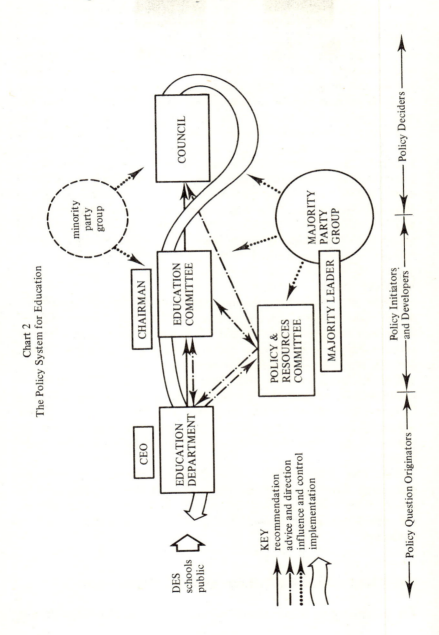

Chart 2
The Policy System for Education

advises the committee on such matters as the effect of the policy, costs and compliance with Department of Education and Science regulations. The committee, through the chairman, may respond with directions to the chief education officer, say, to reduce costs or to make other changes. The chairman may advise the policy and resources committee on aspects of the proposal and may receive directions to bring it into line with authority objectives or some related policy on financing. Influence and control are exerted by the majority party group through the majority leader. This may be informal as when it is known that certain policy alternatives are unacceptable to the group in terms of party aims. It may be more formal as when the group gives directions to the committee and the chief education officer through policy and resources. Control can also be exercised by instructing the chairman and by using the whip when items are to be decided by the committee, thus assuring the passage of party-approved proposals. The minority party group has influence and control too; this is severely limited, however, by the fact that it is out of power, but questions can be raised in committees, and minority members can be instructed on issues.

Much of the recommendation, advice and influence appertains to the process questions, the political and administrative matters for which decisions are requred. The several constraints on the process imposed by various factors and forces such as central control, resources and rates, interest groups and structure of the system are dealt with through these relationships. The questions to be answered and the consideration given to constraining factors are reflected in the way each of the main participants organizes and directs his part of the subsystem and in how he perceives the relationships between himself and the other participants.

The role relationships of each main participant will be examined from his own perspective and the perspectives of others. The chief education officer and the education department are considered first, followed by the education committee and its chairman.

## The Chief Education Officer and the Department

There are three dimensions to their role as chief education

officers describe it. The first is the professional dimension of promoting the service and of planning its future development. The second is that of advising the education committee and the council on policy matters and of executing the policies chosen. The third dimension relates to the political aspects of getting the job done. The three are knit tightly together, and, while deputies and assistant education officers have responsibilities for sections of the service, what they do is directed and supervised by the chief education officer. However, the political aspects are strictly in his hands, as succinctly stated by one, 'I reserve to myself all matters of political persuasion with the committee, the council, the leaders and the policy committee including the chief executive.'

This dimension seems to have become more prominent in recent years, judging from comments by two senior chief education officers. 'Ten years ago my job was thoroughly education,' said one, 'Now I'm sitting here waiting for Labour to put out its manifesto, so that if they take control in May we'll know what we have to do.' The other noted that he '. . . was brought up in the tradition of officer loyalty to his profession'. He went on to say, 'I don't bend with the political wind to get my ideas accepted. I do, however, act as a broker between members of different parties or the same party to get agreed answers from the committee.' Even where parties have not yet taken a strong hold there is similar concern for the political dimension. The chief education officer in one county speaking of his relatively non-partisan council said, 'They haven't given me a line to follow, so I have to drag it out of them and piece it together.' Some chief education officers like this dimension best; some do not like that increased emphasis on politics. 'I like political control,' said the chief education officer in a Labour-controlled authority, 'It means I only have to sell an idea once; then all we have to do is work out the details.' A chief educational officer with a Conservative majority, preferred the professional approach; he said 'I advise the committee on my own initiative, fearlessly and frankly, out of my educational philosophy and best judgement. It may take longer, but I think it is right.' The other four took positions somewhere between these two, and all appeared to be attuned to political control and had developed personal political styles. The necessity for running the political relationships as a part of promoting the service and of advising the committee was evident in the way that chief education officers direct the operation of the education department.

Education departments are organized to respond to needs, to matters of concern and to potential policy questions in the course of managing the service. The focus is on the actions of officers and the questions and reactions of elected members. This is facilitated by an organizational structure which parallels the education committee structure. Each of the various principal officers, deputies or assistant officers is delegated a measure of responsibility for day-to-day management of a section of the service and is professionally responsible for its improvement. A principal officer, designated by the chief education officer, works to each subcommittee which supervises a section. However, proposed changes, requirements for funding, requests from members and emerging policy matters for that section, whether resulting from central government directives, local problems or the officer's evaluation, are taken up with the chief education officer.

In each of the six authorities officers were expected to initiate changes in their sections and to sort out questions that should go forward. Chief education officers expected their assistant officers to develop procedures and regulations for their sections within approved policies. Most assistant officers said that there were no limits on their making suggestions or getting advice from colleagues. In the main, such consultation is concerned with management problems and coordination with other sections of the service. These consultations also help in the identification and definition of questions to be taken up with the chief education officer. Subordinate officers soon learn what they may act on and what to refer even under changing conditions. One assistant officer said, 'I was brought here to build buildings. In that, I have great freedom to work with the committee. Part of my task was to devise a scheme for locating secondary facilities that abets going comprehensive.' He indicated that the basic policy direction had been worked out by the chief education officer and the committee, and any attempt by subcommittee members to avoid or confound that policy direction in implementing the building programme '. . . is immediately reported to the chief'. In another authority, an assistant officer remarked, 'With the election a few months off and control of the council hanging in the balance, everything goes to the chief education officer. Members are concerned about a lot of little things, and the chief does not want their political nervousness to upset our progress.'

An important activity in proposing change is the 'floating' of an idea with the committee. This is a delicate operation, combining the professional dimension with the political. Chief education officers monitor it carefully, working informally with an individual officer or perhaps more formally through the directorate. Two approaches seem to be used in starting this. An officer may consult with colleagues and may present his idea in a memorandum or report to the chief. Alternatively, the chief education officer may request that an idea be studied and may direct an officer to initiate interoffice consultations and to prepare a report. Next, there is a political test applied by the chief. As one assistant officer described it, the test has two parts, 'First, does the idea fit within the broad aims set by the majority and can the officer cite the text (e.g. manifesto, previous policy actions)? Second, what nod, wink or specific request did we get in committee?' If the test results are positive, the idea may then be 'floated' in a report to the committee and reactions of members examined. There would, of course, be a prior check with the committee chairman before placing the item on the agenda.

Failure of an idea to pass the test or an unfavourable reaction in the committee does not mean the abandonment of an idea. If its educational merit is sufficient, it may be furthered through that dimension of the chief's role which concerns the future development of the service. As one chief education officer noted, 'You nibble away at things, planting seeds and creating climates for their growth.' In this longer-range aspect the deputy or deputies can play a vital role in conjunction with the chief education officer.

The post of deputy education officer is one which the chief can use to delegate a number of functions or none at all. About the only set task of a deputy is to deputize for the chief education officer when he is out of the authority. Apart from this, a deputy may have a particular assignment spanning several sections of the service such as finance and administration or research and evaluation. He may be one of the two or three deputies responsible for coordinating the work of assistant officers in broad areas such as planning and development, resources or schools, or for supervising the implementation of approved aims and policies. Often the deputy is a clearing-house for ideas to be taken up with the chief education officer. He reviews memoranda and reports prepared by assistant officers, pointing out weaknesses or suggesting additions and says whether or not an idea is ready for the chief's action. If an idea is accepted for development, the chief may hand it over to a deputy to get the job done. When the chief wants to initiate an idea, he and his deputy divide the work. The deputy takes the educational development as his task, while the chief plies the committee chairman and other members. 'Everyone in the department knows that I speak for the chief in doing such work,' said one deputy, 'and while I'm getting them to put together the report, they know I have the chief's assessment of the political side, and they do not have to raise those problems.'

Perhaps the most important role of a deputy is that of a confidant to the chief education officer. If the chief and his deputy are personally compatible the confidant role develops around two aspects, a personal alter ego for checking views and a professional equal for private exchange of ideas. A certain formality remains, however: the chief has the final choices and retains a hold on all political matters. 'I hear about things first,' said one deputy, 'proposed changes, political moves. He can tell me because I keep these confidences. I respond with my observations which I know won't be spread around.' A county chief education officer revealed that he and his deputy had met nearly every morning since reorganization 'to figure out what we should do to survive the day'. No division of their duties had been made, and they simply had to decide who would be most effective in which areas, until the department settled down. Part of what was being determined was the impact of the transition from one party to another as their 'political masters'. On the professional side, one chief said that he and his deputies like to lay aside political problems to discuss matters which are strictly educational. They do this once a month over dinner, ranging through selected topics for future attention and development. As one deputy said, 'The politics will come along later. What we try to do is to get out our best professional thinking.' Of course, no one around the department believes that 'the junta' is not discussing the politics of education.

Many of these department activities, information about committee matters and proposals, are included in the chief education officer's directorate or staff meeting for discussion and possible action. It does not seem that chief education officers use these meetings to resolve courses of action for themselves. Rather, the directorate is a gathering point for opinions, for questions and for the issuing of further orders. If a report needs more work, the chief requests that it be done. If a particular political situation has changed, the chief informs the officers thus—if he feels it is necessary to their work. He may also inform them of the actions he has taken and of items to be sent to either the coordinating subcommittee or the main committee.

The relatively tight organization and direction of the education department provides the chief education officer with two things essential to his effective performance, information and time to conduct the external relationships of the department. When he combines this with his understanding of the general directions and aims of the controlling party, the chief truly exerts the political dimension of his role. However, the basis of his role remains his professional expertise supported by the information available through his operation of the department.

Two main participants with whom the chief education officer is most concerned are the majority party leader and the chairman of the education committee. They are means of approach to the majority party group and to its decision processes. There is also concern about monitoring and influencing the policy and resources committee. There are two central purposes in these relationships: to promote and advance the service through advice and recommendation and to keep himself informed about the aims and objectives of the majority. Chief education officers rely on the chairman to be their main political conduit. Contacts with the majority leader are secondary, but the development of policy and resources committees may be giving these contacts greater significance.

*The Majority Leader*

All six chief education officers described their contacts with majority party leaders as usually informal and not too frequent. The primary objective is, as one chief said, 'To see that the leader gets information similar to that which the committee is getting, in the hope that his views will be based on that information.' It did not seem to depend on the relative influence of the chairman in the party, whether weak or strong, nor did it seem to depend on the leader's attitudes towards education, whether sympathetic or not.

One county chief education officer, with a chairman of little experience and a neophyte in party politics, met with the leader about once a cycle. These meetings were always cleared with the chairman, and the discussions focused on contentious items between the parties, new ideas and intended directions of the majority. In a London borough, the chief education officer had a strong chairman but felt it highly desirable from time to time to 'persuade the leader, to teach him and to explain some of the deliberations on education'. In a county where the majority leader supported education, the chief consulted with him mostly on new central government directives, relying on the chairman to carry other messages. Another chief who felt that the majority leader was not at all sympathetic said he occasionally communicated with him on important items but other than that did little more than 'pass the time of day' with the leader, leaving most matters of persuasion to the chairman. Direct contact is not always necessary, and chief education officers admitted to using several ways of informing and obtaining the views of party leaders through others. Among those mentioned were members of the group policy committee, the chairman of the finance committee and, occasionally, the chief executive. The responses, including the directives, are mainly referred back through the committee chairman.

Majority party leaders tended to have the same views about the contacts with chief education officers—informal, not too frequent and usually initiated by the officer. Leaders prefer to have technical professonal information directly from the chief education officer, especially when it concerns Department of Education and Science circulars or regulations. Occasionally, they said that officers require information about procedures to be followed, e.g. whether an item is going to be referred to the policy and resources or the service committee first. Leaders have a distinct preference for giving political directions through committee chairmen, but they do not hesitate to reinforce these with officers if it seems necessary. This seems to depend more on the leaders' judgements about the nature of the issue and the professional view of it than on any strength or weakness of the chairman. If the chief education officer has to overcome a professional bias in working to party aims, he may be given a special briefing, The reverse is also true: the chief education officer with the chairman, may request a meeting with the leader to make the professional's concerns clear. Party leaders, it seems, are sensitive to the importance of relationships between chairmen and officers when extra effort is needed to move the chief education officer.

As for the leaders of minority parties, chief education officers say that they keep them informed on what is happening, e.g. where matters are with the committee, as one put it, '. . . much as I would with any member who enquires'. In three authorities, this was not difficult as the minority party leaders were on the education committee. In two authorities, it was more critical because the minority leaders felt that with their small numbers their best people were not on the education committee and that the leaders had to keep abreast of education's concerns in order to direct the activities of their party in a better way. The *quid pro quo* for the chief education officer is information about minority aims which he tends to stockpile, in order to understand what will happen in the committee but also against the day when the minority may become the majority.

## The Chairman

The chairman of the education committee is a dominant force in the life of the chief education officer because much of the political dimension of his role develops around the relationships with the chairman. The chairman's is important in two ways: he is education's representative in the party group and with other committees, especially the policy and resources committee; he is also the person from whom committee members tend to take their lead, majority members on all matters and all members on non-party non-political items. The political representation aspect arises from his experience and the expectations of the party as to the responsibilities that chairmen should carry out. Leadership with the committee rests on his knowledge and interest and the fact that members often do not take time to study matters for themselves. To chief education officers the two aspects seem equally important if their advice and recommendations are to be effective.

Chief education officers study their chairmen carefully to learn their strengths and weaknesses. The chairman's style and ability to handle the task are judged in order that the chief education officer can keep the relationship productive for both. After assessing the chairman, the chief education officer often sets out to remedy weaknesses that could be detrimental to the chairman or the service. The optimum is to have a balance between the chairman's interest and leadership and his representational role with the hoped-for result of a chairman who is reasonable, supportive and loyal.

All chief education officers noted that chairmen must be politically oriented if the representational aspect is to be effective. None felt that a chairman's influence within the party was of first importance, although it seemed to be more desirable to have an influential chairman rather than to have one that was not. Their point was that chairmen must approach their work through the aims of party and the need to retain political support for the service rather than as people interested in doing things for or in education. As one chief education officer said, 'My chairman has to be made independent of the officers and to look at things from other perspectives. Party control is tightening, and my briefings have to be turned into politically acceptable statements by the chairman.' Another felt the same, 'If my chairman can't define the line between the councillor and the professional, we're both in trouble.' Both of these officers had new chairmen, but the same problem exists with more experienced chairmen. At times, a chief education officer has to remind his chairman of political pitfalls in taking a certain tack in order to know that he understands the risks. 'I arm my chairman as best I can,' said one, 'His group will give him a bad time and will tell him I sold him a bill of goods unless he can counter as to where the proposal is consonant with party aims.' This does not mean that chairmen take political cues from officers, but it does mean that professional views require a political setting to be supplied by the chairman. If he needs help, the chief education officer should be astute enough to provide sufficient hints and advice.

On the leadership side, chief education officers want chairmen to be interested in and knowledgeable about the service, especially with regard to the magnitude of resources required and the problems to be faced in moving such a massive service. It does not mean detailed understanding of how the service is operated but sufficient knowledge to be confident that the chief education officer and the department are managing the service effectively. Interest should extend far enough to perform the full range of chairmanship duties including the necessary public appearances. All six chief education officers had had experience of chairmen who delved too deeply into details, but only one reported that his current chairman had that weakness. 'The chairman will learn,' he said, 'we've problems coming that will preclude members' hands-on actions.' Keeping the chairman out of management areas gives further rewards. A chairman who does not get involved in details does the best job of keeping other committee members out of them.

Other aspects of leadership in the committee are doing the necessary reading of reports and other homework, controlling discussion without dominating the committee and keeping the various subcommittees on some reasonable schedule. By doing his homework a chairman can reduce the number of questions he has to direct to the chief education officer in meetings; constant reference is a weakness in the view of some councillors. Letting members have sufficient opportunity to talk brings out any differing views, but dominating the session is bad, because members often feel it is a sign that the chairman is just pressing home the officer's recommendations. Keeping the subcommittees on schedule is a time-saving which shows members the chairman's grasp of questions. However, chief education officers usually handle agenda development and give their chairmen advice on coordinating the work of subcommittees.

Chief education officers agreed that the best relationships with chairmen could be characterized as informal, open and mutually supportive. By informal they mean that each should feel free to call on the other between meetings. It may be a question about which the chief wants some reassurance on his proposed course of action where delegation to him was not clear. For his part, the chairman may want to indicate that he has heard of some incident in a school and that the chief ought to know. No approbation is attached either way. Openness is a sharing of information and understanding. For example, if the majority is suddenly going to abandon a proposal from a subcommittee, the chairman tells the chief the reasons. If the chief education officer is having difficulty with a board of governors, he can outline the problem fully and politically with a request that the chairman should take appropriate action within party circles. Mutual support is the ability of one to count on the other to do his best within his role. For the chief education officer this includes relying on the chairman to keep the committee majority focused on the problems at hand, to move proposals and requests through group meetings and to endorse officers' actions which, even though unpopular, are taken in line with approved policy. For his part the chairman expects the chief education officer to be trustworthy, i.e. he expects his advice to be well thought out, but he will do what the majority decides even when he disagrees.

Having examined the education department and chief education officers perceptions of his relationships with majority leaders and committee chairmen, the discussion now turns to the education committee and the viewpoint of the main participant, the chairman.

## The Chairman and the Education Committee

Education is considered by many to be a strong semiautonomous service of local government. This is regarded by most chairmen to imply a greater responsibility than that which falls on other service committees, because there are few real checks on education within the formal structure. They tend to see the committee as responsive within a larger scene, setting directions which take into account public pressure, community good and professional advice. At the same time, however, none denied that this is done within a political frame provided by the majority party.

### Members and Officers

Chairmen divide their role into two parts, working with the committee structure and members and conducting the relationships with the officers and party leadership. The division is not as hard and fast as chief education officers perceive it. To quote one chairman, 'It is a very complex job, but the heart of it is keeping officers and members harnessed together.' Problems cited by chairmen seemed to illustrate his observation. Some members fail to involve themselves in committee work, leaving opportunities for cliques of a few members to form and press for certain solutions regardless of officers' recommendations. Such cliques are often based on sectional interests or the desire to change the financing for local service provision. When too few members contribute, officers tend to proceed in their own directions with what one chairman called 'professional momentum'. Then there are councillors who believe that their reelection depends on accomplishing successful case work for their constituents. According to one chairman, 'These parish pump politicians promise what they can't deliver. They try pressuring the officers or getting influential members to pressure other members. The chairman has to stop them, and in that he may need the leader's help to see that they are exposed in the group.'

There are worse problems. Party leaders and chief executives believe that more young well-educated active people are being elected to local councils. However, few want to serve on the education committee. One vice-chairman said, 'Education has declined as a social service frontier. Members see more important decisions and more good things to do in other areas such as housing and social welfare.' The result is that education is obtaining experienced but less active and interested councillors. These members are inclined to leave the work to the chairman and the officers. The trend is not universal; one county chief education officer believes that at reorganization he acquired a more management-oriented hard-questioning young middle-class committee.

Another problem is the increased amount of politics in education issues and the haste to imprint party labels on every action. This was quite obvious in two county councils where hard party politics arose with reorganization. It was also true in an Outer London borough where a strict Tory faction has taken over from a moderate group. The effect is to push subcommittees into divisive political stances, whereas chairmen believe that a squaring with political aims should be carried out in the coordinating subcommittee or the main committee. As one chairman noted, 'Flexibility and the chance to compromise is lost, officers become discouraged and the coordinating subcommittee has to undo the mess.'

The coordinating subcommittee is a screening and monitoring device, according to chairmen. It controls what will be assigned to subcommittees and what will go forward to the main committee. The technical side, the consolidation of reports and the advice on resource needs, is left in the hands of the officer who is responsible to the committee, usually the chief or a deputy. The political side is the chairman's province, and control is exercised through referral of items and recommendation or denial of funding requests. In the five authorities which have coordinating subcommittees and in the county where the main committee coordinates, there are *ad hoc* meetings of subcommittee chairmen to reply to political matters and to give further directions. Only one chief education officer said that he attended these essentially one-party meetings, but all said that they sent in briefs if requested. The chairman in the Labour-controlled county had doubts about these sessions for that reason, 'We discuss the very things on which we need professional advice. Political questions come up only because the group hasn't sorted out its aims properly.' However, other chairmen felt that the one-party meetings were desirable because reevaluation of the political scene may require modified directions. 'We have that freedom, and it is better for the service than going back to the group,' said one Conservative chairman.

The relationship between chairmen and chief education officers recognizes the fact that the committee should have both political and professional leadership. It also recognizes that in doing so they have interdependent but separate roles. Chairmen stressed a shared knowledge of the service as a measure of interdependence. Sanctions against use of politics in a certain way by the chief emphasized the separation that chairmen felt was desirable.

All six chairmen believed that it was their obligation to reach some parity of knowledge about the service with the chief in order to be effective. All expressed confidence in their chief education officers as professionally knowledgeable and loyal, although one chairman added 'cantankerous' to his description. No chairman seemed to feel overawed by the expertise of the chief nor saw this as a barrier to his gaining knowledge. 'Certainly he has the upper hand; he deals with education questions every day,' said one, 'but a chairman who's doing a proper job will learn enough to get on.' This theme was echoed by others. Another, thinking of his task with members, said, 'You have to know enough to ensure that the officers are giving sufficient information to the committee.' There was no hint of mistrust here but rather a reflection of the expectation held by members, the party group and the chief that a chairman will learn enough to understand the advice and recommendations of the officers.

Most chairmen think that their chief education officers educate them through briefings, through working in committees and through contacts on questions which arise between meetings. But as one chairman said, 'It isn't complete, until you begin to pursue things on your own.' The chairman who described his chief as 'cantankerous' felt the same, 'He was telling me where he is professionally, and that forced me to find out where I am on education as a Conservative chairman.' It is doubtful that many chief education officers are that rigorous in educating their chairmen.

The other basis for effective interaction is political understanding. There is a clear expectation on the part of every chairman that the chief education officer will not engage in politics without the advice and guidance of the chairman nor will he attempt to involve the chairman in political ploys. This applies regardless of the strength or weakness of the chairman, his position or influence in the party. Using a powerful chairman to outmanoeuvre the committee or the leader is disapproved of just as much as taking advantage of a weak chairman to press a proposal through. The reason is obvious: if the chairman is expected to represent education in the party group and the policy and resources committee, he has to be sure of the political situation. The implication is that the chief must have a good grasp of each political situation in order to determine when his role gives way to that of the chairman.

Most chairmen think that it is unnecessary to educate chief education officers in politics because the career of the chief has thoroughly prepared him to work closely with politicians. What seems to be necessary is the delineation of party aims and directions in particular situations, explaining the context in which decisions will be made. This is where several chairmen felt that they had problems. 'If the group doesn't set some objectives, I find it difficult to advise the officers,' said one. Others did not seem to feel limited by the group and were comfortable with making their own interpretations for the chief education officer. To some extent these chairmen seemed to have more experience and more influence in their party than chairmen who found it difficult to advise. Yet, one chairman, new to county politics and who had never before served on an education committee, believed that the easiest route was for him to bend political situations to meet education's ends. This was a matter of persuading the group and the leader to change their perceptions of certain constraints at least as far as education is concerned.

## The Party Group and the Leadership

A committee chairman's relationships with other committee chairmen, with policy and resources and with the majority leader all revolve around his role in the party group. While the basic role is that of a representative for education, there are different aspects to its conduct. In the party group, with other chairmen and with the majority leader the chairman tends to be an advocate for the service. In policy and resources, the aspect of defender of the service seems to be more prominent. The explanation probably lies in the expectation that chairmen will put forward their service in the party group and will receive approval from the group for their proposals which will put party aims into action. Party approval is assumed in policy and resources; thus it is the questions of requirements and claims on resources as proposed by the committee which have to be defended in competition with the requests of other services.

The relationship between a chairman and his group depends on three factors: a convention which gives him reasonable freedom to act, an understanding that he will share knowledge and information and a trust that he will not thwart the wishes of the party. The convention operates because the group approved the selection of the chairman, and he almost invariably has the backing of the leadership. The knowledge of the service which a chairman possesses reinforces this freedom because rank-and-file members do not have time to study the problems themselves. Sharing then becomes important in the sense that members' enquiries will be answered to their satisfaction. The expectation that chairmen will not thwart party wishes reflects the idea that the group is paramount. However, if there is no party preference or previous position, the wishes of the group are hard to ascertain. To some extent, chairmen in putting forward their service and as advocates of it, help to define party wishes.

The first rule for chairmen in the party group is an ancient and honourable rule of political parties: there must be no surprises, i.e. the group should be given notice that a question is to be presented and that decisions are to be taken. This holds whether the item is a committee recommendation or a new dictat from the Department of Education and Science. There is some allowance for emergencies, but the chairman is responsible for demonstrating his lack of prior knowledge. The second rule is equally binding: to be able to inform colleagues of what is occurring in his committee and to explain the actions that it is taking. This is a responsibility which cannot be shifted to other committee members or which cannot be excused by any failure of the officers to inform the chairman fully. Chairmen reported little difficulty with these two rules because chief education officers keep them well informed about service needs and emerging requirements. The information is given informally to the majority leader as soon as the chairman and the chief have determined that the authority ought to consider action. Proposals under development are also included as report items, thus preparing the group for further committee requests and recommendations. Together with current items that appear on the council agenda and related questions, proposals are covered by the chief education officer in a briefing to the chairman before the group meeting.

Chairmen usually say that they have no difficulty with items going up to the council. The groundwork has been done, and with a briefing the chairman can move the committee report through. 'To some extent it is a farce,' said one Labour chairman, 'You get repeats of the same arguments heard in committee, but it's all agreed in the end.' A Conservative chairman had the same impression, 'No one really wants to refer back an item. They may vent some anger, but it's all too late.' There is the occasional embarrassment when a recommendation does not seem quite ready or is thought to be too weak to stand up to a council debate. The chairman and the leadership may then decide to withdraw the item.

Getting group guidance on questions and items for future action is more variable. Acceptance of committee views or the reaching of a consensus seems to depend in part on the chairman's relationships with the majority leader and influential members of the party. If the item is a major departure from previous policy or a new directive from central government, there is some discussion for clarification. In the end, such items are referred to the leadership, and what they decide is accepted, according to several chairmen. Discussion of more routine questions is usually limited to the effects on a particular school or section of the community and perhaps the opposition which might be aroused. Often the group leaves matters in the hands of the chairman with the expectation that he will keep the matter within bounds. As one chairman expressed it, the chairman operates within a consensus of group opinion, 'So you listen to the discussion after you present your case and advise the chief education officer on what you think you heard.' The party leader and the group executive or policy committee also listen to obtain a group consensus. The discussion is compared with the advance information transmitted to the leader by the chairman and the chief education officer. If no serious objections or questions are raised, the chairman and the committee are given the signal to proceed.

The same factors of trust, the rules of giving notice and sharing information, which govern a chairman's relationship to the party group hold true in his relationship with the party leader. Apart from this, the chairman's place in the party and his ability to lead the committee majority arise from his ability to gain the backing of the leader and the group executive. Which of these is more critical seems to vary with political conditions in the party. For example, in the two Labour majorities, members emphasized that the education chairmen were influential councillors. One was chairman of the party group and, at least by reputation, a 'king-maker' behind the leader. Given a minority party in disarray on education as well, this chairman had little difficulty in convincing his colleagues that, as he said, 'the proposals for education are drawn directly from our manifesto'. The Labour chairman who said that he preferred to bend political situations to meet the ends of education, believed he had two points in his favour, 'First, I can convince the majority of the committee that the idea is good for education. Second, I can convince the caucus that the Tories wouldn't like it.' He is not a member of the caucus, or clique, but is widely respected in the party because he challenged the caucus's choice for chairman and won. In these instances, the veiled use of power seems to be an accepted adjunct to the chairman's role of leading and recommending for his service.

In the three Conservative majority groups, there seems to be more emphasis on the chairman's ability to lead and control the committee majority. The key word may be dependability. In two groups, each chairman is a member of a 'high Tory' faction which controls one group and is a sizeable bloc in the other. Both consult closely with their leaders. 'It's a matter of staying together on principles,' said one, 'not a matter of getting directions.' In the third Conservative group, the chairman is an Independent turned Conservative, and it is rumoured that a change in party label was the price paid for the chairmanship. It is more likely that the choice was made because the chairman, while a neophyte in party politics, gets on well with both committee Conservatives and Independents. These instances seem to point towards trust in the chairman as a member of a faction. If he can control his committee, the leadership can give approval to committee proposals without fear that the committee and the chairman will exceed their wishes.

As noted earlier, one county authority apparently has no majority party as such. The Independent-Conservative coalition met after reorganization to organize the council. At that time, the education chairman, again an Independent turned Conservative, was asked if she would lead the committee. She accepted with the understanding that she favoured going comprehensive and would take the committee in that direction. It was agreed, but education turned out to be the only committee with fewer Labour members than called for by their proportional strength in council. With the addition of sufficient anticomprehensive members to outvote the committee coopted members, proposals which suggest secondary reorganization can be controlled by the committee majority.

The proposals and recommendations of an informed, dependable and/or influential chairman are generally accepted by the party group. In terms of approval needed to proceed, a consensus may seem to provide a fragile basis, but most chairmen believe that this is the best they can obtain. Endorsement by the leadership does not necessarily strengthen a consensus but rather confirms it. Responsibility still rests with the chairman to keep committee proposals within bounds, subject to further examination by others. An increasingly important source of such examinations is the policy and resources committee.

*The Policy and Resources Committee*

When education committee chairmen were asked to describe their role relative to the policy and resources committee, all indicated that they had to defend and justify the financial requests of the service. Chairmen also reported that the committee had little concern about education policies and plans. They felt that this factor kept the adversarial aspects of defence and justification to a minimum, e.g. argumentation about academic affairs, appointments of heads, school types which did not often take place. Site selection, plans for multiple use of facilities and enrolment projections do become subjects for differences of opinion, because they relate to money requirements. However, most chairmen elaborated on the vast powers available to policy and resources committees for directing and reviewing service committee activities. They seemed to believe that real potential for interference in educational matters exists and could manifest itself at any time. Thus, each chairman to some extent saw his role as one of keeping education items from policy and resources agendas until the chairman and the officers are fully prepared to explain education's purposes and funding requests.

While committee chairmen expressed some fears about policy and resources cutting into the traditional autonomy of education, there was more concern for changing relationships between themselves and the leadership as they direct policy and resources functions. The less in the differentiation of functions between the policy and resources committee and the party group, the less the concern. If policy and resources acts largely as a negative control, e.g. if it denies funds, if it deals with each service request more or less separately and if it tends to accept committee justification mainly in terms of fulfilling party purposes, the differentiation is not great. Three authorities had committees which could be considered in this category: one Labour-controlled and one Conservative-controlled London borough and the Conservative-dominated county.

The relationships between these chairmen and policy and resources tend to be like those between the chairman and the leaders in the party group. The autonomy of education as a service committee is usually an underlying theme. Justification of the recommendation for educational provision is based on information supplied by officers, and often it is the chief education officer who speaks on the more technical points. The chairman may use the committee's record as a defence, pointing out what was done with other monies. Previous promises of support by the leadership as well as committee plans may also be pointed out. These chairmen also seemed to rely on their place in the party and their dependability as chairmen in gaining policy and resources approvals.

In the other three authorities, there is greater differentiation of functions between policy and resources and the majority party group or, as in the rural county, the council leaders. In two authorities, a Conservative London borough and the rural county, the leaders are determined to adhere to the Bains model. Services are dealt with separately within their own terms of reference, but some priority is given to developmental projects and projects undertaken in cooperation with other services. Denial of funds remains as a control device, but at times prior authorization to return for supplemental monies is given to priority proposals. Justifications are sought in terms of previous plans and demonstrated need. Achievement of party objectives may be part of the rationale, but that tends to be accepted as given.

Relationships between these three education chairmen and policy and resources tend to be focused on initiation and response between committees. Because of the viewpoints of party leaders and the make-up of policy and resources, political questions are kept more remote. Autonomy of education may be used as a defence, but that may lead policy and resources to ask what has been done with the autonomy. By using development documents from the department and by vetting the requests, policy and resources presses the service committee to justify and defend its recommendations on the consistency of purposes and the merit in fulfilling those purposes. The information required is that which ties immediate needs to long-range plans and which places a good deal of emphasis on officer–committee coordination. Evidence of wise use of previously authorized funds is stressed: it is the service committee which is reminded of previous promises to perform.

Ambiguity about the functioning of the policy and resources committee seems to be greatest in those authorities where differentiation between it and the party group is greatest. A chairman is more comfortable if he can act the same, if he can present the same justifications and if he can exert the same influences in policy and resources as he can in the group. When he has to change and when he has to rely more on technical and performance information, supplied by officers, to obtain a positive action from his own party leaders, he is concerned. One point made by all education chairmen seems to illustrate their dilemma further. Resolution of conflicts between committees is rapidly becoming the province of policy and resources in all six authorities. For example, in former times, if the education committee felt that the personnel committee had run the service short on, say, the number of positions for groundsmen, the two chairmen would meet to discuss the matter, perhaps to negotiate and to reach an understanding. Now such questions are aired by policy and resources with the decisions being made on recommendation of the personnel subcommittee to the full committee. Procedure tends to preclude much use of influence and compromise; chairmen believe that this is an encroachment on their freedom of action as chairmen.

Party leaders are not oblivious in these matters, but there is little evidence that they are doing much to alleviate them. What does seem evident is tight leadership control, ensuring that a leader who wants differentiation between the group and the policy and resources functions will obtain it. This point will be explored in the examination of the leaders' role relationships which follows.

## Party Leaders

The leader of the majority party may have as many as four roles which he plays in the policy-making process. He can be thought of as the palm of the hand which holds together the members of the majority and the organization of the council. Each role is analogous to the fingers of the hand. First, he is the leader of the majority party group either as its chairman or as the chairman of its executive or policy committee. The second role is that of the party leader in council meetings, the leader for the majority on the floor. He may also be the chairman of the council through which council appointments and procedures are formally conducted. Although convention is against having the leader of the majority fill this post, it was thus filled in three of the authorities

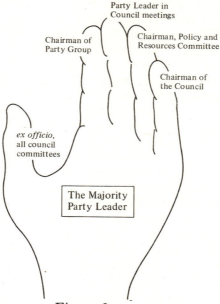

Party Leader in
Council meetings

Chairman of
Party Group

Chairman, Policy and
Resources Committee

Chairman of
the Council

*ex officio,*
all council
committees

The Majority
Party Leader

Figure 2

studied. The fourth role is that of the chairman of the policy and resources committee. Concommitant with one of his roles (and perhaps as the thumb of the hand), the leader is often an *ex officio* member, with a vote, of each council committee. As noted, one authority did not have a majority group as such, but the chairman of policy and resources leads in the council and is *ex officio* on all committees. In this section, the relationships of the leader within the policy system for education are examined through these roles. The emphasis is on the roles stressed by the respondents, the party leadership and the chairmanship of policy and resources. Illustrations of the other roles will be given in conjunction with these two. Minority party leaders are also mentioned in terms of leading their party and of having a seat on the policy and resources committee and also in their relationships with the majority leader.

*The Party Group*

The system of conventions which prevails in the party groups, the necessity of convincing colleagues and the role of the group

135

executive point to one overriding factor, the responsibility of the leader for the political direction of the party. When the party is the controlling party, this has implications for every service. A chairman advocates his service and advises on its requirements. He may also provide views on what committee proposals mean in political terms, e.g. fulfilment of party aims, possible reactions of the minority, effect on the rates and opinion in the community. However, control of the political decisions rests with the majority leader, because he judges the responses of the group and takes advice from the group executive. If a chairman disagrees with the directions he receives from the leader, he can appeal to the party group. However, as one Labour leader remarked, 'We've not been reversed yet.' In the five authorities where there are majority or controlling party groups the leader and the group executive act as the political directorate. 'As chairmen present proposals to the group on what their services want to accomplish, we look at the politics of it,' said a Conservative leader. The task seems to be one of making it politically possible, of finding ways of implementation and of approval rather than of disapproval. Certainly, negative reactions in this dimension would seem to discourage chairmen from carrying out the kind of job that their leaders expect.

What leaders expect of chairmen is easy to state but is not readily observed in practice. First and foremost, it seems that they want the chairman to control his committee and to keep majority members in line behind party aims and programmes. At the same time, they do not want individual councillors to feel stifled so that they have to come to group sessions to say what they cannot say in the committee. Second, a chairman should extract the most from officers; yet, party leaders are wary of proposals which are too costly and which seem to have too much professional polish. They take that as an indicator of officer domination over the committee and the chairman. Third, leaders say that they expect chairmen to pay attention to the long-range development of the service. 'Part of my job,' said a Labour leader, 'is to encourage chairmen to get more and better ideas. Then we can get some real planning done.' However, his education chairman observed, 'Innovativeness is not a qualification for chairmanships here.'

Conservative leaders in three authorities seem to prefer keeping their political problems within the party at a minimum. One, supported by a faction of 'high Tories' which controls the group in a London borough, keeps a tight rein on chairmen. He believes that they must stay together on principles and that committee proposals must reflect those principles. 'I press them hard to come in with things we can support,' he said, 'When it doesn't fit, it goes back to the committee.' This leader believed that the education chairman had managed to keep expenditures down and, though a new chairman, had learned enough to avoid officer domination. In another London borough, the leader has to contend with a strict Tory faction as well as with the moderate Conservatives. While he is probably more sympathetic to the faction, he does not want officers' contributions lost through intraparty squabbling. 'We depend on the officers to move the service, especially something as massive as education,' he said, 'So I listen to the committee reports to separate fact from fiction.' Colleagues say that he is an excellent summarizer and can state questions or issues clearly at the end of discussion, leaving little doubt as to the direction the group should take. This becomes the message which the chairman takes back to committee. The Conservative leader in the county authority achieved broad support within his party through gaining the cooperation of the Independents and through the skilful handling of the Labour minority. 'I propose ideas for such areas as education that I think my party can work with,' he said, 'At the same time, I try to see that they appear palatable to the Independents and to the minority, most of whom are moderate socialists.' Once the group has agreed to the general direction, committee chairmen are responsible for presenting proposals for accomplishment. He was not greatly concerned with the question of officer domination, believing that the committee members are a sufficient check against the capture of the chairman.

The two Labour majorities are different, relying on leadership as enforcers of party policy, while chairmen have the task of getting their proposals accepted by the group. Once accepted, the leader has an obligation to see that proposals are supported by members. The group in one London borough examines major policy proposals through a system of working parties linked to the group policy committee. On some items, the chief education officer is asked in to give his professional opinions. What emerges from a working party is presented to the group as a recommendation of the leadership. Its approval there makes it a party objective and, in the words of the leader, 'tells the chairman what he is to do and puts his committee members on notice that they will follow his lead'. The caucus in the Labour-controlled county sets the agenda for group meetings. The majority leader and the chairman of the group each represent party factions. Subjects allowed for group discussion are only those items which will not cause troublesome controversy between the factions. The education chairman has begun to promote education's interests in this system by having informal sessions with the subcommittee chairmen, thus giving the service a united front across the factions. He would like to have officers present, but, not only is this against their ethics, there is also a fear among the Labour leadership that the officers 'might dominate the council as they did under the Tories'.

Once there is approval, all party leaders say that they support their chairmen by holding individual councillors in line. For example, if a member complains that the new direction is going to affect a school in his area adversely, he can take it up with the chairman. If the chairman cannot or will not accommodate the request, the leader will not usually interfere. 'Sometimes several members will wake up late on a policy proposal,' said a Conservative leader, 'Then they'll want me to get a change made. I tell them to get the group to agree and I will. That usually ends the problem.' Of course, discussion on how an objective is to be achieved remains open, but a chairman who is consistent in his pursuit of means and who appears to be getting the best advice of the officers will be supported by the leadership. Much of this seems to be arranged through informal exchanges of information and advice between the leader and the committee chairman. When it does surface in the group meeting, the chairman can defend the committee's actions. The executive committee will listen too, but usually it lets the chairman decide if his committee should make changes,. As one leader noted, 'The education chairman can hear as well as I can.'

When leaders were asked if the education chairman is ever instructed by the group and the leadership, the responses were mixed. If instruction is defined as telling a chairman to follow certain directions or to make specific changes in committee action, the majority leaders in two Conservative-controlled London boroughs agreed that they instruct. They saw it as a negative control but necessary at times, usually as the result of a group discussion or committee report from which an alternative was chosen to continue on the committee agenda. At other times, the group executive may take an item away for further discussion and may return to the group with a preference to be followed. The chairman has usually participated in the discussion and knows what is coming. In the Labour-controlled borough, if the chairman's ideas of how to reach party objectives do not 'go far enough or fast enough, we'll instruct him', according to the majority leader. This a group policy committee decision based on the rationale that it is responsible for seeing the group's wishes carried out.

The leader of the controlling Conservative group in the county authority does not think he can instruct the education committee in the sense of giving directions on issues and items. The Independents hold the balance of power in the council and must be accommodated. There are few differences in their views on education but overall the leader wants the two groups to be cooperative 'I leave it to the chairman to run the committee within general party policy on education. The chairman has my support and knows I'll keep Conservative councillors in line.' He also works with the Independent leader if the chairman requests such help. In the Labour-controlled county, the leadership has not yet instructed the education chairman. 'Just after we took control a few things came out of the caucus without going through the group,' said the chairman, 'but I just ignored them until they stopped. Now they bring things in and say "please".'

Judgements about what action or reaction might be expected from the minority party as proposals are made also figure in leaders' tasks. Concern for what the opposition will do seems to have less importance for leaders than keeping their own members together behind the party programme. 'After all, 80% of education items are simply concerned with maintaining the service and with showing some progress. These things are non-controversial in the partisan sense,' according to one leader. Similar statements were made by most party leaders. However, when leaders were asked what makes an educational issue into a political issue, they were quick to identify what seems to be a slippery slope. When differences arise over resource need and allocation to money, land and personnel, there is political controversy in the sense of who gets what. As soon as one party takes one side of the question, there is partisan political controversy. 'You look at the context in which an issue arises,' said one Conservative leader, 'and you try to find those points which will allow the issue to be non-political. As soon as someone finds out that money is to be spent here and not there, you get a political division.' A Labour leader felt that pressures from parents or from certain constituencies diverted committees from examining the merits of proposals. 'Then I have to step in, and the other party accuses us of making it a party matter,' he said. Partisanship, the injection of party viewpoints, was felt to be an almost inevitable turn of events as soon as one party begins to believe that the other is trying to gain advantages from the situation.

There is more to it than this seemingly inadvertent slide. The differences in approach to local government which exists between the two major parties are critical in determining whether education issues will become partisan political issues. Every Labour leader that was questioned expressed the notion of party aims and the responsibility of the party for achieving particular outcomes. One summed it up as follows, 'We don't soft pedal our socialism—if we decide we have an aim or an idea of how something should be done, we say so.' By contrast, no Conservative leader mentioned party goals or responsibility as ends in themselves. Their responses tended to reflect only one aspect of the Conservatives' approach to local government—fiscal prudence. As one leader noted, 'On education questions we are accused of being against those things we won't pour money into. There are many reasons for not spending, but emotional people fan these refusals into party political issues.' This implies that Labour leaders have a potentially greater concern for doctrine and party policy in examining issues than do the Conservatives.

There are implications, too, for arriving at political strategies. Labour appears to make mutual interlocking obligations, whilst the Conservatives divide responsibility between the chairman and the leader. A Labour chairman will advise the leader and the group as to his preference for meeting a political situation. He is expected to know the party position and priority for items before his committee and to make his strategy in the light of party wishes. Other members may contribute information about political aspects of the issue and may make suggestions for handling the opposition. For a Labour leader, the discussion becomes essentially a recommendation for political action and, if accepted by the group executive, becomes party strategy. 'We usually accept the advice of the chairman because he has the knowledge and the first responsibility for taking action,' said one Labour leader, 'But, once we've decided, he is then acting for the party, and I have the responsibility to see that he doesn't falter.' Another leader said that he was ' . . . equally responsible to apply the chosen political tack in policy and resources'. A Conservative chairman will also advise his party leader but will tend to define potential solutions in terms of the position and priorities of the committee majority. Other councillors may comment on the solutions, aiding the chairman in determining their viability. For a Conservative leader, the group discussion is more a vetting of the chairman's solutions. 'It is the chairman's job to smoke out the opposition on political moves,' said one, 'then he can get on with committee business.' In this he has the endorsement of the group and the support of the leader for actions to be taken in committee. There seemed to be at least a general feeling towards actions which would lead to compromises between the parties. 'Any majority that is smart will keep conflict down,' said a majority leader, 'If you consult the opposition in the committee and show an amount of give and take, you'll not have political issues tearing up the council.' However, there are limits, and all Conservative leaders felt that they were responsible for making adjustments in political strategy to be applied occasionally in the main committee and certainly in the policy and resources committee and in the council.

The following incident in one authority illustrates Labour's mutual interlocking relationships between chairman, leader and party political strategy. The majority in the education committee had decided on a school site, and it appeared that there would be some Conservative opposition. To make it clear that the controlling party was following its policy of taking officers' advice on sites and of keeping such questions non-partisan, the chairman advised trying to stop the opposition at the subcommittee level. The majority leader, in his *ex officio* capacity, took on the task. 'You heard the chief education officer on this. If we wanted it to be political, you would have heard from the chairman,' he told the subcommittee minority. 'Now I'm here to ask you if you want a school or a fight.'

Similarly, the remarks of a Conservative leader on political matters indicates the party's division of political strategy responsibilities, 'I always say that Conservatives don't have a monopoly on good ideas for education. Well, my education shadow chairman sometimes opposes things when he should be cooperating. I go to the education sessions when certain kinds of items are on the agenda, and I choose whether or not to make them political issues. My group invariably supports me in this.'

Leaders were also asked if they consulted each other on education issues perhaps with the hope of heading off political controversy. Leaders in all six councils said it was rare to negotiate on issues of any kind. Where the majority leader is also chairman of the council, minority leaders believed that they were limited to discussing procedural questions. In the county authority where the Independent–Conservative majority does not have party groups, the Labour leader believes that he gets some small concessions, 'The Conservatives will trade a few sticking points for peacefulness, hoping we won't embarrass them in the council.' Majority leaders of both parties felt that the opposition got previews of the controlling party's proposals through informal conversations and in policy and resources. They believed that they provided sufficient warning so that one party could not accuse the other of springing surprises. Lack of give and take between leaders is apparently new to one county council. According to the Independent leader, critical issues likely to cause friction used to be smoothed over in the members' dining room, 'We used to avoid a lot of noise and fuss in meetings that way. Now they want to fight it out where everyone can hear.'

*The Policy and Resources Committee*

The role of the majority leader and his relationship to the education chairman in the policy and resources committee is not always clear. The degrees of differentiation between the party group and the committee, already mentioned, indicate a range of variability from the simple extension of the group within formal government to the approximation of the Bains model for planning, coordination and management of authority services. One point is clear, however. It requires a strong leader in command of his party group to implement his concept of policy and resources. Councillors are suspicious of a concentration of power if the committee is composed entirely of chairmen and other influential people. They seem to be equally suspicious about sharing power when leaders coopt rank-and-file members onto the committee. Service committee chairmen are even more suspicious in terms of committee control over policy-making, fearing that either power arrangement will cut into service committee autonomy. The result so far has been that majority party leaders have used the policy and resources committee to control the jugular vein of policy-making, finances, and that they have inched their way from there towards their concept.

All majority party leaders agreed that they had done little with education through policy and resources. One Conservative leader who has accomplished at least one long-range planning exercise for the authority believes that it will be '. . . the last bastion to fall'. Another said that it is not education's tradition of autonomy or its statutory existence that keeps policy and resources from bringing it into line for coordination; it is the sheer size of the service combined with its separated structure. There is also the matter of '. . . officers' tight vested interests which adds to its resistance in being harnessed with the rest of local government', according to a Conservative minority leader. A Labour majority leader felt that the group had made progress in ending officer domination by tying education's expenditure to party aims and by insisting on its articulation with other people-oriented services. 'Perhaps in another decade we'll have a chance at planning and evaluation through policy and resources,' he said.

Financing is the key to control of educational policy in so far as policy and resources is concerned. All majority leaders admitted this but, at the same time, denied attempting to extend committee influence into academics, school types or other areas traditionally reserved for the service committee. Yet, failure to provide funds for a comprehensive school or equipment to be used in a new programme was, they agreed, tantamount to making a policy decision for education. Providing funds for nursery education while reducing the amount available for secondary reorganization is also choosing a policy preference. This is more likely to occur in a policy and resources committee which is used as a political instrument of the majority group than one which attempts to promote better management within the services. Under the latter concept, committees tend to trim financing across the board rather than to cut specific requests, and the service committees, including education, may reorder priorities within the funds available to them.

Relationships between the leader and the education chairman

in the two authorities where there is a definite tendency towards the Bains model differ from those in the two authorities where policy and resources is a political control device. 'The task is one of reassuring the chairman that he can get what he needs to operate the policies he wants,' said the Conservative leader in a London borough. 'At the same time, I try to let him know what is required.' There is an apparent strategy to blunt the use of political arguments in policy and resources: items are referred back to the committee for changes rather than amended or reworked for the council agenda. The same is true in the Independent-Conservative-controlled county where the chairman of policy and resources wants a balance of power between the service committee and the policy committee. It seems that the policy and resources committee stays neutral on objectives and tries to be positive about means or plans. There are broad general directions, e.g. keeping the rates moderate, but within those each service committee sets its own policies. Performance review subcommittees already exist in these two authorities. Although they have only checked on interservice cooperation and have scrutinized virement of funds, they '. . . scare the hell out of chairmen,' according to one chief executive, 'because, if you are going to look for an honest airing of performance, the controlling party is going to cut off any retreat to the group'. To some extent, leaders are using performance review as a cudgel so that chairmen will learn to propose sound efficient means to ends rather than to rely on political salesmanship.

In the two authorities where political control is emphasized, the ties between the group and the policy and resources committee have hardly weakened. The leader in the Labour-controlled borough does not believe that they should be separated because policy and resources is the executive of party policy within the government. 'This is where we tell the minority what we are going to do and where we hear their response. If we want to adjust ideas to meet their criticisms, we can. Then, when committees decide, we can all look at the merits and the money,' he said. However, if the opposition will not agree, the controlling party still gets its own way. 'After all, the whole thing is our responsibility and we aren't going to let a service get out of line or waste money.' Thus, a committee chairman has to make his arguments and his defence in the group and in the policy and resources committee both before and after his committee acts. A similar situation exists in the Conservative-controlled borough. The policy subcommittee is a one-party committee that brings decisions out of the group into the full committee. Here, however, the leader says he looks for a match between a chairman's proposals and the officers' recommendations on how to accomplish them. Thus, there appears to be a check on chairmen to determine whether they are getting ideas across to the officers and whether they are obtaining sound plans in return. 'They've got to work together within the financial conditions we face. I think that is the real purpose of policy and resources committees,' he said.

The other two authorities are beset by political problems that are internal to the controlling party which have prevented full development of the policy and resources functions. In the Conservative-controlled county, there is a move in the direction of extending political control through the committee. However, the committee is chaired by the chairman of the council rather than by the majority leader. An elder statesman among Conservative members, he is described as having those qualities traditionally found in council chairmen; a gentleman, fair in controlling debate and not obviously partisan. The problem is that he has extended that role into policy and resources. 'That was a mistake, not making a political choice for the top of the controlling committee of the council,' said the majority leader. 'I shall change that. I shall take that job over soon. Then I can control policy as the majority leader should.' In the Labour-controlled county, rank-and-file members are perpetuating a political division partly out of fear that policy and resources would become an autocratic instrument of the leadership. According to the education chairman, there is a sentiment within the leadership towards a Bains-type committee if differences can be settled amiably. However, if either faction has to make a hard power play to take over, he feels that its leaders would use it as a political weapon to maintain their position, and the fears of the rank-and-file would be realized.

Finally, a word about minority party leaders and their relationships with majority leaders in policy and resources committees. Minority parties in all six authorities have tended to put the leader and one or two influential councillors on the committee. These leaders believe that education has been left with its traditional autonomy and has been treated fairly in financial matters. Several attributed this to the presence of the minority on the committee, 'A check on their power and ambitions,' commented one Labour leader. Another Labour leader in one of the London boroughs felt that the minority learned about plans late but had been able to influence the course of events with acceptable suggestions. A Conservative leader in another London borough was not that generous, 'I don't think they want true consultation with the minority but take our views into consideration when they go back to the group.' Majority leaders agreed with these assessments, noting that they wanted minority support when possible. One added, 'You have to listen to everyone, majority and minority, otherwise policy and resources will be a talking shop instead of a coordinative body for authority activities.'

## Summary

The interrelationships of the main participants in the policy process for education have been presented. The chief education officer, the chairman of the education committee and the majority party leader were singled out as having critical roles which link them together within the subsystem of the committee structure. They make the subsystem (including the party group) a continuous entity. However, it is more than that; the interplay of roles keeps policy-making consistently under political control through conventions and expectations for each role which channel or direct political activity. In addition, there are responsibilities for political decisions and their enforcement. Some are mutual obligations designed to reinforce the decision-making of a participant as he operates his part of the subsystem and to protect the interests of the majority party as decisions are made.

Chief education officers have attuned their roles to the political system and have organized their education departments to move ideas into it. This organization places the chief education officer in command of the activities and decisions which support his role as a political participant in initiation and development of policy problems. Each chief education officer relies on the chairman of the education committee as a conduit into the controlling party and the committee system. The relationship is built carefully because it is the base line in working with the committee majority and the party leadership. Each chief education officer also establishes informal relationships with majority party leaders to ensure that educational matters are articulated with broader party aims. At the same time, he retains a professional independence, available for consultation on technical points and ready to give advice if asked. These latter aspects can be adjusted to meet differing attitudes towards education and degrees of party cohesiveness. However, they do not supplant conventional officer–chairman relationships.

The chairman of the education committee is undoubtedly the linchpin of the system, holding together the professional and political parts through his role interactions. His information about the service and its requirements comes from the officers. His actions in getting through the committee what should be done are subject to the scrutiny of the party group and the party leadership. Keeping one in harmony with the other is a central task, and in this sense he contributes to the development of policy.

All chairmen appear to hold roughly the same perceptions of their task in working with officers, keeping ideas and information flowing to the committee and keeping themselves apprised of what these mean. Differences in their task come in dealing with the party group and leadership. The differences appear to be conditioned, in part, by party approaches to role interrelationships. Labour chairmen are expected to demonstrate the congruence of proposals with party aims. The use of influence or position in the party to get a consensus is an accepted practice. From a consensus, leaders and chairmen derive mutual obligations, each within their own role, to carry proposals through. The task for Conservative chairmen revolves around the demonstrated dependability in adhering to party principles and in controlling the committee majority. Then the proposals advanced can be endorsed by the leaders and the group. Once endorsed, chairmen have leadership backing within the committee, although ensuing political decisions are reserved for the leaders. The difference is critical because, while chairmen of either party help to define what should be done through the advocacy aspect of their role, Labour chairmen have the added necessity of meeting a political feasibility test.

The role of party leaders was cast in political terms, e.g. when in the majority they have the responsibility for leading the group towards the attainment of party objectives through organizing and directing the efforts of members in deciding policy. In this sense, the majority leader may be considered a policy-decider. Leaders expect chairmen to obtain the required professional advice from the officers but to avoid officer domination. They expect chairmen to control their committee majorities and to advise on political strategy. For Conservative leaders, there is an inclination towards accepting, in so far as possible, the committees' terms of reference as conditioning political decisions, thus leaving the chairman room for only limited manoeuvre. For Labour leaders, application of the agreed party line seems to take precedence, the group providing the terms of reference.

Party leaders use policy and resources committees to achieve financial control over authority activities. Service committee chairmen are placed in the position of being defenders rather than of being advocates of their proposals. They rely on officers to provide technical information on which to build these defences. Although education chairmen felt that the service had not been adversely affected by the advent of policy and resources, there was concern about the changing relationships between chairmen and leaders. This is particularly true where leaders have blunted chairmen's political influence through a concept of policy and resources which clearly differentiates it from the party group.

The following chapter combines the roles of the main participants and the structure of the local education authority in the dynamics of the policy process. The examination will be developed using the six-stage process model introduced earlier.

# 6 The Policy Process for Education

This chapter is designed to bring together the roles and inter-relationships of the main participants, the constraints and the structure for policy-making. The six-stage policy process model is used as a framework in order to locate and identify decision points. At each stage—initiation, reformulation of opinion, emergence of alternatives, discussion and debate, legitimization, implementation—the considerations made and the decisions to be taken by the policy-makers are presented. The intent is to determine, in so far as possible, who makes which decisions and, perhaps more importantly, who influences the decisions of others. The constraints on the process, the structure of the committee system and the imperatives of political control also have a bearing on the determination of who makes which decisions. These factors will be seen as reasons for certain decisions being taken and will help to explain the actions or reactions of policy-makers. Again the responses of members, officers and others are used to illustrate various points.

## Initiation of the Process

There is unanimous agreement that policy-making begins with the officers, particularly the chief education officer. Through their contacts with schools, boards of governors, teachers' organizations and their own observations, they identify discontents and needs. Department review of case files or financial reports may indicate that new policies are desirable. There are also letters from parents or school associations and interest groups asking what action the authority is taking about some aspect of educational provision. Another source is the individual councillor following up case work for a constituent. There are also clues from the committee and, more directly, requests for reports on various topics. In some situations, an officer will investigate to determine how widespread the problem is, and he will begin preparing a memorandum, reporting his findings and perhaps suggesting the need for a policy.

The process is also triggered by Department of Education and Science circulars, requiring authorities to meet some new national policy or regulation. These go directly to the chief education officer for study. He will usually direct an officer to examine the decree and to report on the implications for the authority. Additionally, an interpretation is requested from the chief executive's legal staff.

The process also begins when the majority party wants a policy to deal with a matter identified in the party manifesto or to fulfil an aim set out in accordance with doctrine. Initially, this requires examination within the department as to the potential effects on existing policy and provision.

Chief education officers declared that few things broke on them suddenly. As one noted, 'More often it is the opportunity that opens up and that you have to be ready for if you want to get things done.' Obviously, officers follow what is being discussed at the national level and watch local elections with interest. The routine information-gathering by the department is a continuous activity. The task of the chief education officer is to collect things together so that he can take advantage of opportunities and, more importantly, so that he can set about creating them.

Each chief, to some extent, uses the directorate meeting as a clearing-house for prospective policy problems. Two use additional means, closely involving their deputies. In one county authority, it is 'the junta' through which the chief and his three deputies sort out items for further development by the department. Another relies on his deputy to sift items, returning some to the department for administrative solutions or more information and sending others on for action by the chief.

The final selection of problems and policy matters for development is made by the chief, looking forward to the initiation of proposals within the committee system. Each item is roughly cross-referenced for its political and educational implications. The first consideration seems to be the educational dimension and how certain policies would fit into the future development of the service. 'Political choices tend to be short-term choices,' said one chief education officer. 'I have to think about where we'll be ten years from now educationally. I don't want political solutions that box in the service.' There is evidence that all six chief education officers held this same view: without exception each was in personal command of any question that was about the reorganization of secondary education. The next consideration is political and concerns the general mood of the committee. 'You have to determine how far they will go with an idea and, if conditions are right, to ask for the resources,' according to one. The same questions are raised about policy requests from the controlling party. 'They usually don't send anything solid, so I give them a measured response, feeling my way along,' said the chief education officer in a Labour-controlled authority.

Once selection is made, the department continues the development of information within the broad considerations made by the chief. He, in turn, informs the chairman on emerging ideas, preparing him for the questions which might be raised and obtaining his early reactions. The process has been initiated, but firm proposals for policy will not be made by the chief until he has explored the political climate through consultation. His purpose is to extend his professional influence into the process far enough to ensure that educationally viable policy alternatives are not foreclosed by political decisions.

## Reformulation of Opinion

The second stage of the policy process is critical in determining the directions which policy proposals will take. This is the stage where party political matters begin to merge with educational matters. It appears to be almost exclusively an exchange of ideas and opinions between the chief education officer and selected majority party members, i.e. there is a marked absence of direct input from those persons and organizations who might be interested, even those who expressed dissatisfaction or who requested a policy change. The chief education officer is the pivot between educational and the political interests, the political dimension of his role becoming most evident at this stage. His relationships with the chairman and the majority leader are most important as he considers which ideas will be 'floated' with the committee and which will be given review by the party group.

This stage divides into two parts, opinion-gathering and opinion-making. In both parts, consultation is a central activity. According to one deputy, it is 'genuine to-and-fro consultation', because of the obvious risk in misreading opinions which could lead the chief into a position where he undercuts his chairman politically. Conversely, if the controlling party misreads the chief, it may find that he has set a course that cannot be effectively accomplished by the department, and thus this may produce political repercussions.

### Opinion-gathering

The chief education officer gathers opinions through consultation with the chairman and, perhaps, other members of the committee. Occasionally, he will meet members of the party group's policy committee or the majority leader. This is a testing time as various department ideas are put forward against party views on education. Not only are ideas tested for fit with known party positions but also with potential constraints which councillors believe might affect proposals at later stages. This includes costs (because they might rebound on the rates), reactions of teachers and other interest groups and the general concern which might be raised in the community. At the same time, the chief is questioned about possible costs, about when he thinks policies might be needed and about what the effects might be in the authority's educational provision. Much of this is carried on informally, perhaps over a period of several months.

Consultation with the majority leader at this point would occur if the chief education officer has questions about a party request for policy. If the costs seem disproportionately high or if the chief has difficulty reconciling the request with the long-range development of the service, he informs the leader. 'If what they want won't work, I find it best to tell the leader early on,' said one. 'It saves a lot of grief.' Others agreed, noting that cost factors are the most frequent cause for alarm. The chairman is told first, of course, as otherwise he may have to explain to the group why he did not warn them about the expense entailed. The outcomes are either a reworking of the majority's idea or a decision to seek a scaled-down version as the chief may advise.

For a given area of endeavour, the chief education officer probably has considerable knowledge of the special interest concerns of many individuals and organizations. If he feels he needs further information, he has to devise a way of impressing his need on the chairman in order to begin consultations. This presents problems because chairmen are quite reluctant to let such consultation begin until there is a consensus within the party on the directions to be taken. Most chief education officers agreed that their best chances for outside consultations at this early stage were to confine them to somewhat controllable situations. For example, school governors can be asked if it is felt that they have something to contribute. With teachers, the joint consultative committee is available. Other advisory committees for special areas might also be used. Individual councillors of both parties may be contacted informally, although only two chairmen, both Conservatives, said that they would not object if the chief education officer wanted to consult a member of the minority. However, there seems to be a strict taboo on consulting with interest group leaders, even if they are coopted members of the education committee. Several coopted interest group leaders affirmed that they are consulted only in the committee, after policy alternatives have been chosen.

*Opinion-making*

Opinion-making starts almost simultaneously with opinion-gathering. The targets are the party group and the leadership. With the tentative department ideas taking shape, the chief education officer determines when and how to 'float' them. According to one, the purpose of the political test—the identification of a 'nod, wink or specific request' from the committee—is used as a check on 'the progress of members' thoughts as I have shared my thoughts with them'. The objective of the chief is, at least, to prevent dogmatic decisions and, at optimum, to create opportunities for presenting a range of policy alternatives for examination by the committee. Delay gives rise to rumours, and so another objective is to put ideas before the committee as soon as possible after the questions have been raised.

The committee chairman will usually work with the chief in the opinion-making task. They share the same perceptions of it and once the chairman is persuaded to move in the direction that the chief has indicated they may share the activities. It is not difficult to persuade a knowledgeable supportive chairman on the educational merit of ideas: all chairmen were confident that officers do not propose outlandish schemes. The essential concern of the chief education officer is that he does not get ahead of his chairman in the political aspects of opinion-making. While the chief tends to operate from the technical-professional end of a persuasion continuum and the chairman from the political end, a chief's personal style appears to determine how far he will extend his activities towards the political end. The one imperative is that he must keep the chairman informed of what he is doing.

Proposals clearly acceptable to the majority and essentially non-controversial require very little to smooth the way through to opinion-making. All chief education officers thought that they benefited by attaching, whenever possible, such new ideas to policies which had already been approved. This incremental approach saves time. With the chairman's agreement, items can go directly to the appropriate subcommittee in five of the six authorities. Incrementalism is an acceptable tactic with Conservative majorities, probably because of their tendency to rely on the judgement of the chairman in handling the committee. It is more risky with Labour majorities because habitually informing the group after the fact is not acceptable behaviour for a chairman.

There are two distinct situations where opinion-making is essential: changes in policy areas known to be contentious between the parties and potential departures from the political opinion of the majority. The second situation includes ideas which the majority wants developed but which the chief believes require modifications. More importantly, it includes new ideas which the chief education officer wants considered as advances in the service, ideas which he believes have sound educational merit. The decisions in these situations are political, and opinion-making by the chief brings the political dimension of his role into full play.

Two chief education officers rely on their chairmen to do most of the persuasion, well within the usual conventions of officer-chairman relationships. In the Labour-controlled county, the chief shares information and opinions with the chairman. He, in turn, builds up consent with influential members of the majority factions so that he has support before the caucus. 'I bend what the chief education officer provides to suit conditions as I find them,' said the chairman, 'Then I tell him what adjustments we may have to make.' It is the same in one of the Conservative-controlled London boroughs where the chief presses the chairman to pass all ideas to the committee quickly. He has even been known to ask the minority leader to complain when the majority keeps questions bottled up within the group. Both officers place high priority on getting ideas into the committee with as few restrictions as possible. This speedy strategy takes advantage of the education committee's place in the structure and its traditional autonomy.

The same strategy is used in the county authority where there is no majority group as such. The chief and the chairman make informal checks with influential members of the education committee, inform the chairman of policy and resources of their findings and put the proposals before the committee. From this activity, they obtain an approximate idea of the political line that is likely to be taken by the committee majority.

In the other Conservative borough and the county authority where the Independents hold the balance of power, the efforts of the chief education officers are focused much more on obtaining the group's acceptance of what is new. The chief in the Conservative-controlled borough directs a steady stream of information to the majority leader. When department ideas are put forward which require the majority to go against its aims, the chief is known for quietly 'buttonholing' members in addition to taking his case to the leader. The chairman follows this by gathering reactions and by advising the chief on what is thought of these ideas. In the county where the Conservatives dominate, the chief education officer consults with the influential Conservative and Independent members. He tends to keep within the broad party aims which the Conservative leader has for maintaining the alliance with the Independents but stresses the implications of various ideas for different areas of the county. His chairman does the same, following his briefings. Both of these chief education officers rely, in part, on their relationships with their majority leaders. They also rely on the fact that both leaders are averse to limiting officers' opportunities to propose ideas.

In the Labour-controlled borough, it is altogether different. The party group or, more accurately, the group policy committee predetermines its directions through its advisory committee structure. When the department proposes new departures for the service, these are also taken to the group leadership for examination. The chief takes his ideas to the chairman, and they attempt to predict the response that might be made by the leadership. They do some opinion-making with one or two members of the group policy committee and the leader. If the results are positive, the chairman puts the ideas on the agenda, and the chief will often be invited in for the discussion before the committee reports to the group.

Department of Education and Science circulars receive separate treatment on their way to the group in these authorities. The educational and financial implications are shared with the chairman, together with the legal advice obtained from the chief executive's department. While all six chief education officers send in written summaries, only three said that they send in advice, and only one of them said that he occasionally makes recommendations as to what course the authority should take. The majority leader may want a briefing in order to make a recommendation to the group. This would be important to the chief education officer as he might obtain an early indication of the majority response. The basic decision is a party decision, but in the long term the leadership will have to depend on professional advice and the chief's ability to conduct consultations with the Department of Education and Science. As one said, 'If the majority won't accept my advice, I may have someone in the Department of Education and Science go over the matter with the chairman. If they still want to do less or do it differently, they will get my best efforts.' Opinion-making is less visible, perhaps because the controlling party will ultimately have to conform.

The joining of educational ideas and political directions takes place in the party group. In five authorities, the controlling party asks each chairman to outline what he intends to accomplish with his committee. This is done at group sessions devoted to policy planning and what is decided determines the aims of the party for the next few cycles. The party leadership sums up what has been done since the previous meeting and indicates some general directions especially in finance. They may also mention major changes in central government policy when they affect local government. Then chairmen begin their reports, to be followed by group discussion.

The education chairman proposes the ideas developed and tested through opinion-gathering and opinion-making. The group compares what is outlined with the party philosophy, the national party policy and the local party manifesto. More importantly, previous accomplishments and expenditures by the committee, as well as difficulties, are reviewed. Party leaders and members agreed that the group invariably approves the general outline of the education package with few modifications. In two of the three Conservative majorities, the group executive may give some prior endorsement to the chairman's proposals or may state a preference for an amendment as discussion opens. Chairmen in all three say that further directions are occasionally given, based on the leadership's assessment of the group discussion; according to one leader, 'It's never anything you can't deal with in the committee'. Labour groups give the impression of being more directive and of exercising greater control over committee proposals. The caucus in the county authority may delete an item from the agenda if they have not come to agreement about it. If questions are raised by the group, the committee chairman is asked to take them into consideration by the leadership and to let them know the response of the committee. In the Outer London borough, the policy committee reports to the group by presenting its views on education proposals and by having the chairman amplify and explain. If the questioning reveals weaknesses or raises too many problems, the policy committee will take the proposal back for further discussion. The usual result, however, is that the chairman is told to proceed to the committee with the proposals as approved by the policy committee.

In the two London boroughs where the policy and resources committee is used as a political control device, there is a further review of proposals following the gaining of a group consensus. The Conservative majority looks at the funding requests and the implications of any reorganization of service provision. It will set a limit on expenditure for the guidance of the education committee. The Labour leaders do not limit spending but insist on knowing how the chairman plans to control costs.

The party response to chairmen's proposals seems to be almost anticlimactic. As one vice-chairman put it, 'My party agrees as lambs, follows like sheep', in such discussions. The few changes suggested are given to the committee for consideration. At first glance such results give opinion-making the appearance of being overdone; however, opinion-making has purposes which extend beyond this stage. One of these purposes is to prepare the group for the specific alternatives which will come from the education committee as recommendations.

## Emergence of Alternatives

The next stage, emergence of policy alternatives, centres on the education committee and its subcommittees. The objective is to set out different approaches and possible policy solutions where members and officers can examine them. Another purpose is for the majority party group to reach more definite decisions about its direction in the light of the options presented. Department of Education and Science circulars are in this category, as the education department's summary is reviewed and the advice of the chief education officer is considered. This stage is also important in the timing or pacing of policy-making. Because it takes place almost entirely within the government, there is ample opportunity to control the steps to be followed within the committee system. However, as the process moves towards discussion and debate, individuals and organizations from outside the government can begin to erode that control by pressure for consultation. As might be expected, the controls are political, and the chairman of the education committee becomes dominant at this stage.

### Professional Proposing

Chief education officers and committee chairmen agreed that it is the officers who provide the policy alternatives for committee consideration. Proposals are embodied in the officers' reports and are scrutinized by the chief. He chooses the alternatives to send forward. These are usually discussed with the chairman beforehand, and the extremes are eliminated by comparing the 'practical aspect' with the 'principle' as gleaned from the consensus of the party group. How the alternatives are chosen and whether or not the chief recommends one alternative over others is a matter for considerable judgement. As one noted, 'This is the art of the possible, and I like to ride the right horse going in.' The right horse, it seems, is a curious-looking beast. Each alternative must be one that the department can carry out effectively with the resources which will be most likely to be made available and yet which will still be consonant with the aim and direction that the majority party has approved. The proposals should look firm, i.e. they should be based on available information and should spell out what the effects will be if adopted. On the other hand, they should be flexible enough to bend when members' questions imply a need to accommodate particular situations. Appropriate alternatives will be acceptable to the controlling party, but any one alternative can be abandoned without political embarrassment if necessary. Finally and quite pragmatically, the proposals must leave something for the members to do, to make a contribution in reaching a policy.

Direct formal recommendation of one alternative over others by chief education officers is surprisingly infrequent according to their own admission. Chairmen do not look favourably on recommendations by the chief, as they believe these tend to lead the committee and to preempt discussion. As one Labour chairman put it, 'The choice of an alternative to pursue is a majority decision.' Another chairman, a Conservative, said that, if the chief education officer wants to make a recommendation, it must be cleared through him. A recommendation as such may be unnecessary. Members indicated that it is not difficult to determine the one that the chief favours. Taking a different perspective, one chief education officer said that few officers would propose alternatives that they would not endorse. Of course, there are always informal recommendations to the chairman, as he steers various alternatives through the committee system.

The notion that the choice of an alternative is a majority party decision signals a marked change in who is doing what in political persuasion. The education chairman becomes the central political figure. As policy proposals become more specific, he will have to respond to members' questions both in the committee and in the group. As other alternatives are proposed by the minority party, he will have to keep his majority in line. If the minority develops an opposition to the majority proposals, the chairman will have to advise the party leadership on political strategy for handling the situation. The chief education officer emphasizes his professional role, supplying information and 'keeping the chairman from plunging along party lines when the questions get tough', as one minority spokesman put it. His task is to see that educational interests do not become submerged and that the chairman moves the discussion in the general direction indicated by the group consensus, the base on which his alternatives rest.

Referral of items to subcommittees for study and recommendation is the task of the chairman. He consults with the chief education officer in making his decisions. What must be considered are the speed at which it is desired to arrive at a policy, the control of the range and scope of alternatives and the degree of exposure to be given to a question. The assumption has been that the lower down in the system an item is sent the less the interest the majority party has for controlling these factors. For example, special subcommittees and working parties were thought to provide opportunity for a greater range of alternatives to emerge through the participation of coopted members, teachers and other selected contributors. Exposure would be maximum, as the participants sought the opinions of their colleagues and association members. The assumption may no longer hold. In one county authority, a special subcommittee on secondary reorganization, according to the education chairman, 'has initiated nothing and its members spend all their time watching each other'. In one of the London boroughs, the minority leader believes that working parties are usually overloaded with friends of the majority. Officers in all six authorities feel somewhat better about special subcommittees and working parties if they have a high proportion of teachers, advisors or inspectors serving on them. Of course, referral of an item to the full committee or the coordinating subcommittee at this stage is taken by the minority as a sign that the majority group has already decided the question and that the chairman has his orders to push it through. The regular subcommittees receive most items because of their continuing role within the structure and because of their amenability to whatever degree of majority control that is deemed necessary without making special arrangements. Here, too, party control appears to have tightened generally, with subcommittee chairmen keeping in close contact with the chairman of the education committee.

The convention has been that partisan politics should not intrude heavily on subcommittee deliberations. Minority party leaders and education spokesmen say that this convention is being eroded rapidly. In the Labour-controlled London borough and one of the Conservative-controlled boroughs the policy alternatives proposed by the majority are the only ones given consideration. 'The best we can get is their reconsideration in the group,' said the Conservative minority leader, 'Sometimes I can get a minor change made in policy and resources.' The Labour minority leader said, 'We are left to poke holes in what they offer. All we can do is repeat our objections in the full committee and in the council.' In the other Conservative borough, the minority spokesman believed that the officers were their only salvation: 'In subcommittees they may reinforce one of our suggestions with the chairman. Then it will get considered. This never happens in the main committee, however.' The minority leader in the Labour-controlled county noted that alternatives which might appeal to the Conservatives are cut off and that they are left to suggest only small modifications. The Labour minorities in the other two counties say that their proposals receive consideration but are not often accepted as substitutes. In the Conservative-dominated county, there is the danger that the Independents will not go along with 'socialist ideas'. The Labour leader in the other county said that requests for higher spending or those related to speeding up secondary reorganization are eliminated.

When asked if majority members contribute other alternatives for discussion, committee chairmen were almost unanimous in agreeing that they do not. In the county where there is no majority group, members from certain sections occasionally offer proposals designed to suit their interests, but these are laid aside. A Labour chairman indicated that his members were not really knowledgeable enough about the service, nor did they have time to develop genuine alternatives. A Conservative chairman said that a few members from one or another part of the borough sometimes combine with coopted members to push an idea but, 'if it looks like Labour and Liberal are interested, I knock it down'. Majority members often attempt to amend items in order to obtain favourable treatment for their wards or to display their ability in acquiring special treatment. 'Most of it is vanity,' said one Conservative chairman, and it has to be treated the same as minority efforts to 'string questions together in a fashion which implies an alternative'.

Subcommittees, then, are confined to discussion of the alternatives proposed by the officers and endorsed by the chairman. This does not mean that real changes cannot be made or that there will not be any agreed recommendations to go forward. Members say that they are free to raise questions and to suggest modifications. These may deal with costs, effects on particular schools, comparisons with other authorities and expected reactions of parents and teachers, as well as with the department's plans for implementation. Such matters have to be separated and examined in the light of what the officers know of the situation and of how far the chairman believes that he can alter it without losing control. If inequities will result or if unexpected obstacles are found, amendments will be considered, or several alternatives may be modified into one proposal.

Officers respond to many of the questions, providing information requested by members. Responses are carefully controlled, i.e. they are technically correct and are just sufficient to answer the question. Opinions are rarely advanced unless they are requested and unless the chairman gives permission. Some chief education officers are worried at having to exercise a 'gate-keeping' function at this stage. One said that he disliked his officers 'giving answers that aren't answers' just because a full response would give the majority a problem. Another felt that hardening party lines were reducing the candour which should characterize the professional's contributions, preventing effective 'brokering' to achieve agreed recommendations. Chief education officers prefer to negotiate, adjusting priorities and shifting funds on the basis of educational needs rather than bargaining for a consensus by satisfying members from one area to gain support for another activity. Chairmen try to keep blatant political bargaining to a minimum, but the constraints under which subcommittees work do not permit it to be eliminated entirely.

There may be consultation with other interested persons or organizations at the subcommittee level. This seems to arise out of a need to estimate reactions or the desirability of giving notice that a particular situation is under discussion. It does not seem to be consultation in the sense of reaching joint agreement but more in the sense of informing and listening. It is selectively undertaken in order to avoid creating controversy and possible resistance. For example, if a particular school is to be affected by one or more alternatives, the chairman will contact the councillors from that area and perhaps will ask the chief to obtain reactions from the governors or from the parents' association. If Department of Education and Science reactions are required, the chief education officer will be directed to make inquiries. If there are to be changes made which will require action by another council committee, the education chairman will inform the other chairman of the tentative direction of subcommittee discussions.

Subcommittee discussions result in decisions to recommend one or more alternative policy proposals to the main committee. The subcommittee chairman, the officer who works to the subcommittee and perhaps the chairman determine when there has been sufficient examination of any question. They review the points raised and calculate which alternatives and modifications will receive the most support. Officers say that votes are not often taken in subcommittees, the preference being for a consensus. On partisan issues, the minority may want to be recorded as opposed to the issue, or they may agree while putting the majority on notice that they intend to continue opposition to certain points in the full committee.

### Political Choosing

The next set of process decisions are made within the majority party. The *ad hoc* meeting of subcommittee chairmen, the coordinating subcommittee and the majority party group interact as the political hinge of the policy process, adjusting the alternatives to fit the party aims. It is the chairman's job to convince the group and the leadership that the recommended alternatives embody the party's wishes. In other words, he has to convince the group that this is what they wanted all along. The chief education officer will help the chairman to sort out items and to see that the majority leader receives any further information he should have before the group meets. The chief will also give the chairman a briefing before he goes to the group. One thing is clear; the chief supports the alternative or alternatives recomnended by the committees, and, while he may suggest minor changes to the chairman, it is rare for him to attempt to thwart the wishes of the majority by continuing to press for an alternative which he favoured.

Recommendations from subcommittees are first reviewed by an *ad hoc* meeting of the subcommittee chairmen and the chairman. This procedure is followed in all six authorities but only in one, the Labour-controlled London borough, does the chief education officer meet with them. While political factors influence the categorization and disposition of items, the purpose is to prepare for the chairman's presentation to the party group or, where there is no majority group, to the committee majority. Officers and members agreed that there is an effort to keep proposals in the committee until the chairman feels there is a consensus among the majority members which will be reflected by their support in the group meeting.

The first category is financial, and recommendations connected with requests and allocations of resources are referred to the coordinating subcommittee. The second category is for items which might be contentious within the majority party. If there are sectional interests or ideological divisions to be faced, the *ad hoc* meeting might keep the item off all agendas until they have explored ways of gaining a consensus. Then the item could be referred back with directions or could be sent on to the main committee. Third, items which are contentious between the parties are, in most cases, taken to the group. A strategy for handling the opposition is devised and is given as advice. Finally, non-controversial items are nodded through to the full committee.

In the five authorities which have coordinating subcommittees, the chief education officer advises the chairman on the make-up of the agenda. Consideration is given to the handling of financial problems. Chairmen reported that these fell into three types. First, the cost of carrying out the recommendation is higher than expected. Second, some member or clique of members has slipped in an exception or addition which is costly. Third, the recommended alternative is not articulated with some existing policy and requires further expenditure under the existing policy. Several subcommittee chairmen and party leaders believed that the officers were often at fault and that their expansionist tendencies coupled with their control of information permitted the ballooning of costs. Chairmen disagreed, fixing the blame instead on the laxness of subcommittee chairmen in 'letting members talk too much'.

While some items with financial problems are referred back, most are straightened out in the coordinating subcommittee. Both officers and chairmen believed that this is a more effective procedure. However, if it nullifies an amendment pressed through by members of his own party, the chairman has to make sure that he conveys this information to the party leader before the item comes up in the group. The same holds true if the coordinating subcommittee agrees to additional spending. Conservative chairmen feel that their leaders expect them to explain changes to their committee majority and to make them stick. Labour chairmen were more inclined to ask for the help of the leadership.

The closing of the political door takes place in the majority party group, led by the group executive and advised by the education chairman, it commits the majority to specific policy proposals which it believes embody party objectives. When this choice is made, the party leader becomes the central political figure in the policy process for education. The discussion of proposals under development is conducted as a series of comparisons between what is being proposed and what the party position ought to be. The chairman is responsible for demonstrating the congruence, although members consider it to be 'open season' on all items and for whatever points they wish to raise. Once a consensus is achieved, the group has to decide how to make it politically possible. The leadership determines the options available, and, as it will have the responsibility for the political strategy, the group simply tends to ratify the choice.

When the education chairman reports to the party group, he relies heavily on the opinion-gathering and opinion-making which he and the chief education officer have done earlier. If the leadership and influential members have been kept informed and if committee deliberations are going in the general direction which the chairman indicated he wanted to go, whatever the chairman proposes receives approval. Where there are differences and where alternatives do not match party wishes as defined through group discussion, the chairman will be under notice to bring the proposals into line, or he will even be instructed to make specific changes.

In the Labour-controlled London borough, it is a matter of convincing the leadership that the recommendations of the group policy committee can now be realized if it follows the alternative that the chairman is proposing. Tight control over alternatives up to this point assures that proposals mainly follow the predetermined directions. Where the chairman and the chief education officer believe that greater funding will be required or that a delay is desirable, the chairman makes a case for those modifications. 'Sometimes that can imply a different policy,' said the leader, 'It's up to the chairman to prove it isn't and then to ask us to change our priorities.' In a Conservative borough and the Conservative-dominated county, comparison centres on any endorsements or amendments put up earlier by the leadership and the committee proposals. 'The two aren't always congruent,' said one leader, 'but, as long as there are no great disparities, we'll endorse the one the chairman wants.' The disparities which members believed caused trouble were too high a cost or an inadequate application, e.g. too many exceptions or an over-abundance of services to a particular section of the authority. In the London borough the leader is sensitive to sectional concerns and accepts greater variation across the community. Neither leader felt that he had ever opposed or had ever led the group executive to oppose the chairman's recommendations, but modifications are suggested in keeping with the 'promised aims of the party' or to meet a specific problem which arose suddenly. Majority groups in the other Conservative borough and the Labour-controlled county are the least rigorous in their examinations of developing proposals but for different reasons. The Conservative majority leader concerns himself with two factors: are the estimated costs still within the limits set in policy and resources, and can the education department carry out the policy? His standard question to chairmen indicates this, 'Did the officers say it can be done?' Priorities are sorted out later by the leadership in the one-party policy subcommittee of policy and resources. Unless there are political problems, the group approves education's recommendations. With the Labour majority in the county authority, if the chairman has support across the factions, approval is a foregone conclusion. Apparently, the needed comparisons are made, and a consensus is determined in a premeeting of the caucus, but the responses of party leaders offer few clues as to the comparisons they make.

Simultaneously, political questions are raised. Some are intra-party, while others deal with the expected position of the minority. Chairmen say that this is the most hazardous part, because they have to prevent unanticipated questions or emotional pleas from interfering with committee progress.

Members, chairmen and leaders agree that it is difficult for a clique or an aggregate of councillors to modify committee proposals substantially. First, there has been consultation with those members whose wards or special interests are affected. Where necessary and desirable, their interests have been incorporated; otherwise they have been told why such matters cannot be met. This information has been conveyed to the leader. Second, the committee majority is prepared to squash changes and amendments. The result is that members ask for more specific details, criticize some past action or suggest an unfavourable community reaction. 'In part, you depend on the leader to detect meddling and to separate the reasonable question from the unreasonable ones,' said one chairman. The unreasonable question has to do with specific steps in implementation, relocation of personnel and distribution of monies to certain activities. Members complain that they need these facts to make decisions but are increasingly told that such management problems are best left to the officers. If a member feels that a policy might adversely effect his ward, it falls on him to make a case for wanting to go against party aims. The best that he can hope for is a suggestion by the leader that the chairman might look for some adjustment.

Questions about how to deal with the other party or parties also arise. While few set strategies were indicated, there is a tendency towards accommodation. Compromises on non-controversial non-partisan items, made in subcommittees, are accepted as reported. When responding to Department of Education and Science circulars, majority leaders say that they keep the other party leader informed about intentions, but minority suggestions have to be examined in the committee, the same as with other issues. A degree of openness for modification is maintained so long as the minority accepts the basic choice of the majority. The implication is clear: it is probably better to have minority participation than opposition. It is contentious items between the parties that cause the most difficulty.

Controlling parties do not seem concerned about whether

minority parties become a focus for dissatisfaction in the community. The ability of factions of the majority, scattered third party or Independent members, coopted members and even governors and teachers to create dissent within government is of far more concern. Thus all five controlling groups tended to look at minority positions in terms of their attraction to members who might side with the minority or others who could resist the majority's wishes. Education chairmen say that they would like more freedom to incorporate modifications and to make adjustments which would blunt minority objections. Their groups seem unwilling to give that much freedom. Labour is particularly stiff. 'Members are sure some Tory shadow is going to outsmart you,' said one chairman, 'so they try to lock you in.' Conservative chairmen felt that they had some room for further bargaining, and they try to list for colleagues the points which might be conceded if minority support is desired in order to prevent the accusation of arrogance.

Labour leaders said that members and chairmen were bound by the group decisions. They expected chairmen to keep their committees close to the party line and to use the whip when there is sentiment for a minority proposal or negotiation. No Conservative chairman said that he really wanted to use the whip in the committee, but all felt that the chairman should be able to decide if it is necessary rather than having to make the leader decide. Conservative majority leaders were adamant: to use the whip in the committee or anywhere else is a leadership decision. It rests with the chairman to demonstrate the need. 'Otherwise, some of these chairmen would use the whip to conceal their own weaknesses,' said one leader.

By fusing a proposal to political aims, the controlling party has chosen the policy it intends to put through the main committee and the council. It has also sketched a political strategy. The task in the discussion and debate of the policy process is to defend its choice, as it begins to be more explicit about what the policy will mean and how it will be implemented.

## Discussion and Debate

This stage can begin almost as soon as the policy alternatives are first examined in a subcommittee, and it can continue through the council meeting when the policy is ratified several months or cycles hence. On the other hand, discussion and debate might be a flurry of activity crowded into a fortnight before the education committee meets to legitimize the decision of the controlling party group. In so far as some interest groups are concerned, discussion and debate takes place between the parties: it does not reach out to include members of the public. Certainly, on many items the majority and minority are in agreement, 'and there is little in these basic technical matters which could be of concern to the public', to use the words of an Independent leader. However, it must be said that on contentious items between the parties and on proposals which the chief education officer and the chairman agree should be selectively tested outside the government, there is discussion and debate which includes the public.

Consultation is a central activity of this stage, when the process expands to involve people and organizations in the community. It is a very different kind of consultation from the sort that was observed in reformulation of opinion and during emergence of alternatives. It is not designed to seek a consensus of opinion nor to inform, i.e. to elucidate intentions. There appear to be two purposes which depend on how the question is put. First, there is the gathering of reactions and opinions when the question is as follows, 'What would you think if the authority established a policy to do so and so?' Second, there is the gathering of suggestions in anticipation of implementation when the question is the following, 'How do you think the authority might best proceed if it establishes a policy to do so and so?' It appears to be artfully done so that, while the officers and members sift and weigh what they hear for the purpose of adjusting proposals or of making implementation decisions, the majority is not committed to specific suggestions. Seeking support from the public and from interested organizations does not appear to be a primary objective. The consent-building that is done is almost an extra dividend. It is reflected in the factors considered where participants are chosen to aid the department in implementing policies. Those who are thought to be supportive and, in addition, who offered some reasonable ways of proceeding are most often asked for this later consultation.

Who is consulted and why does not seem to take any regular

pattern. The choices are made by the chief education officer with suggestions from other officers. The education chairman may also be asked who should be consulted. Officers tended to agree that who to consult and for what purpose is decided from their experience. As judged from officers' responses, consultation with teachers has a high priority; consultation with individual school associations and persons or organizations that previously expressed concern about the topic have the next priority, then organizations in the section or geographical area most likely to be affected and also those with a known general interest in the question. Before initiating consultation, the chief education officer informs the chairman. This is obligatory if he plans to contact teachers, governors or known opponents of what is being proposed.

Consultation outside of government is not popular with elected members in spite of strong pressure from the Department of Education and Science. There are several reasons for their negativism. First, many feel that the public can contribute little to the technical side of policy, and more normative interests have already been expressed through the ballot box. Second, some items are considered strictly the province of the council, e.g. Department of Education and Science circulars. This is rationalized by saying that the local education authority is an administrator of central government policy. Third, councillors, as part-time servants of the people, say that they do not have time for additional meetings. On the other hand, several chairmen considered participation as part of the job; one Conservative said that he held more than 60 meetings during his first year as chairman, and a Labour chairman said that he always took part if the chief asked him to attend. Only one majority leader, a Conservative, expressed an opinion on participation by the education chairman. He felt that education attracts active people who cannot be ignored, making it important for the chairman 'to get out and to get their views'. Chief education officers were ambivalent about including chairmen. If governors are involved or if a panel of councillors meets with a panel of teachers, they would prefer to have the chairman participate. If it is a teachers' panel only or a school association, the chief would rather have only officer involvement.

Interest groups in local authorities work hard to discover ways of being consulted. Access to officers and members is open and easy. Interest groups often express their views, but that is quite different from being asked. Ideological alignment with the majority party is of some help, but, apart from that, home-school federations and units of national organizations devise other strategies. The favourite methods seem to be organized letter writing directed to councillors to create a semblance of widespread interest, followed by the secretary or a small delegation calling on the chief education officer. Another tactic is to get several groups from different school units to ask for a joint meeting, and, if the department responds, the visiting officer is then faced with a panel of interest group leaders. When councillors have to be reached, it is majority members who attract the attention, because it is obvious that the controlling party is the only viable target. Efforts are focused on reaching the chairman of the education committee with the hope that he will suggest the organization for consultation. Interest group leaders reported that majority leaders were often informed of organization wishes.

The results of consultation are collected in the department. Some responses are formal. Joint consultative committees send letters in addition to minutes containing recommendations. Teachers' organizations also file letters. It seemed to be currently popular to use referenda when school associations and others feel that consultation has not sought opinion fully or when they want to make a record. In one London borough, parents of pupils in Church of England schools asked to be surveyed on continuation of secondary provision under church auspices. One county authority was asked to hold a referendum about a school going comprehensive. Parents felt that the 'old boys' had taken over the meeting, overshadowing the opinions of parents. In both instances, the education committee was reluctant but followed the suggestions of the leadership to hold referenda. While the chief education officer undertakes interpretation of consultation results and advises the chairman, modification of proposals is a majority decision.

Turning to the minority party, leaders indicated that there were two strategies available to them at the discussion and debate stage: seeking modification of majority proposals in the committee and, barring that, exposure in the committee and in the council. Concessions which might be made by the controlling party are made in the subcommittee, but, unless it is a noncontroversial item or an issue where the majority wants minority support, further modification is hard to obtain. Strategy is made in the minority group, and as it is political strategy the leader and the group executive decide what it will be. The committee shadow chairman advises the group on what might be effective. Getting the chairman to yield a few points before the main committee meets is sometimes possible if he has not been instructed. Reaching the majority leader is fruitless except for arranging some procedural delay. The result is that the minority is left to choose whether it will let committee members go along with the majority, whether it will try to get a few further changes or to begin with a party stance aimed at exposure or whether it should be forward-looking and hope to have some effect at implementation.

Minority leaders said that such decisions take into account the views and opinions of constituents, school associations and interest groups, in so far as they are known. However, the basic decision is made in terms of what the party feels it ought to do within the government. Most minority parties do not take their objections to the community, seeking support for their stands. Discontent over a majority proposal will be used if it is related to matters which concern the minority party. For example, in one authority, the Conservatives switched from a neutral position on a church school question because they felt that the majority had not given sufficient consideration to parental rights. There is apparently little solicitation of those organizations and individuals who might be opposed. Only one minority leader, a Labour member, reported doing this, 'On education questions particularly, I write or telephone every one I can think of who might be against what they (the majority) are proposing. I ask for letters and then unashamedly use these to embarrass the Tories.' Consultation with constituents is not systematic, either. If there happens to be a school or neighbourhood meeting in a member's ward, he might speak if invited. If the purpose of the meeting is to hear from an officer, the member knows because he has been informed by the department as a courtesy, but courtesy demands that the member should not take up political issues with an officer.

When asked if there were attempts to align teachers' organizations with minority positions or to reach coopted members and governors with the minority message, party leaders said that they did not. Of course, a governor friendly with the minority and on the board of a school affected by an impending change of policy might have some impact with parents. Teachers' unions as individual organizations might file an objection which is useful, but, as one minority spokesman put it, 'Teachers have too much at stake in the joint consultative committee to ally with the minority. We can and do amplify complaints we hear if they fit with our line of attack.'

Minority leaders believed that the strategies they devised and that the information they collected during the discussion and debate stage had to be considered in the light of later steps. In the committee and in the council the majority resolves political conflict with its votes. As one leader put it, 'They get their way and we get our say.' Apart from that, the minority may have an opportunity to influence the implementation of policy.

Within the majority party there is also discussion and debate. Members receive constituents' questions about proposed policies and usually refer these to the education chairman. The volume of inquiries is not large except on major issues such as going comprehensive. Chairmen pass inquiries to the chief education officer for response to the councillor and for use in determining community opinion. Although no officer said that he kept track of the number of letters inspired by minority positions, all said that they watched for trends in particular wards or sections. Such information can be used when implementing policy, if there is a choice of where to begin, and it becomes a part of the summary prepared for the chairman as the legitimization stage begins.

## Legitimization

Ratification of majority proposals is a three-step progression: the education committee decides and recommends to the council; policy and resources reviews the committees' requests and recommends to the council; if the two recommendations coincide, the council ratifies the policy. Given the fact that the majority is likely to have its own way, the important decisions are those made in the committee premeeting and the approach taken in policy and resources. The concern faced in each is largely political and whether or not to use the full power of the controlling party. The majority leader remains the dominant political figure.

The way this stage will be handled depends in part on the

assessments made by the chief education officer and the chairman. The results of consultation and inquiries are consolidated by the chief; the political situation both intraparty and *vis-à-vis* the minority is summarized by the chairman. Their purpose is to determine which questions will cause difficulty if left unanswered and which points might be open to modification without detriment to the policy. There is some give and take between the two. 'He may want to make an exception or to cause a delay because of some complaints,' said one chief, 'but, if that will present problems in the department's application, I have to tell him.' Conversely, if the chief education officer wants to emphasize an element of the proposal that the chairman feels will cause discomfort for some members, he will ask the officer to reduce his emphasis. Other small modifications may be made to demonstrate that those who were consulted were consulted in good faith. The result will be that the chairman prepares to accept limited amendments in committee.

Political questions of more significance, where there are indications that some majority members or allies may break, where coopted members are upset with what they heard in the community or where consultation indicates rising controversy when the policy is implemented, are reviewed by the majority leader. The preference of party leaders is to get the decision made and to resolve political conflict at the committee level. The clear expectation is that this will be done in accordance with advice or directions received from the group. If changes are proposed, they have to be explained by the chairman. If these are not satisfactory, the leader may suggest holding the item for further group discussion, or he may tell the chairman to proceed and to take the risk of political repercussions. Consideration is made not only in terms of the education committee but also in terms of the effects in the policy and resources committee and in the council. If it is a matter of money, too much or not enough, the leader may be willing to let that difference go through the committee and to make a correction in policy and resources. Chairmen also say that their leaders do not want to 'pick up the pieces'. It is on this point that the decision to use the whip is made if it seems essential to pull the committee majority together.

The one variation is in the county authority where there is no majority group. The leader is informed of potential problems, but what will occur in the committee meeting is not controlled in the absence of group directives or the whip. The chief education officer feels that members are not averse to letting the full council resolve the political conflicts, 'There is no history of parties here, and, without a party line to follow, the majority is always willing to let conflict go on up.' The chairman is slowly obtaining the subcommittee chairmen's agreement on finances, but there is still too much unpredictability in the committee according to the chief. This means that a decision in committee might be reversed in the council.

Committee premeetings are used to assure that the committee session will go according to plan. The chairman and the chief review the agenda, noting which changes can be accepted. If there are anticipated problems within the party, the whip will have already been issued. The chairman may decide to have all majority members at the premeeting and then caution them against giving way to pleas or provocations by coopted members or to the minority's attempt to exploit the majority's difficulties. At times, the meeting is rehearsed right down to who will speak and on what topic.

Approval of majority proposals by the committee constitutes a recommendation to the council as required. The next step is review and recommendation by the policy and resources committee, a recommendation that will go to the council. At this step, committee chairmen change from role of political advocate and advisor to that of defender of the service. He becomes more dependent on the chief for technical information, while political decisions remain in the hands of the majority leader.

Party leaders agreed with chairmen on the chairman's role before policy and resources: he has to defend and justify what the committee proposed. 'P and R can't change committee objectives,' said one leader, 'but it can suggest it doesn't like them well enough to fund them fully.'

Denial or reduction of funds is based on a negative report from the finance subcommittee of policy and resources after it has reviewed the planned expenditures. Although the officers draw up the financing plan, the chairman has to provide the rationales which tie finance to objectives and to demonstrate what one leader called 'a consistency of purpose'. Judgements are made by members, other chairmen, who have heard the general outline of education's programme in the group. The proposal is also compared with long-range plans and past accomplishments.

In the two London authorities, one Labour, one Conservative, where policy and resources is used as a political control device, the leadership focuses on the match between earlier education proposals and present education recommendations. There is also some examination of agreement between authority policies on resource allocation and education's requests. Adjustments which are made are based on the leaders' assessments of what is needed or on their political judgements of what is necessary. Items are occasionally referred back if the required change is more than a matter of funding or if it seems desirable to have a positive committee response. Changes in finance are often made without reference to the committee. This leaves the problem of readjustment to the committee because it deals with the implementation of policy. Appeal to the party group is possible but is not often made because policy and resources is the executive of party policy.

The policy and resources committee in the Labour-controlled county and the Conservative-dominated county tend to act in this way also. Differentiation between the committees and the party groups has not become clear, so that there is a bias towards political control in so far as it will further the truce between the factions for the Labour majority in the one and it will maintain the alliance with the Independents for the Conservatives in the other.

In one Conservative-controlled London borough and the Independent–Conservative-run county, the leaders believe that policy-making is a service committee function. In both authorities, new departures, personnel needs and funding requests of education are vetted in the policy and resources subcommittees. If the results do not seem to agree with previous plans of the education committee or with authority fiscal policies, questions are raised in the full policy and resources committee. Items which cannot be justified by the chairman are referred back. In the county, comparisons are made with development documents required by the estimates. In the London borough, ten-year plans were developed by each service in 1969, and, though made inoperable as total packages by rising costs, they are used as reference material by policy and resources. A dissatisfied chairman in this authority can go back to the group with an appeal from the policy and resources decision. However, appeal is of limited use because there are many rank-and-file councillors on the subcommittees of policy and resources who are selected by the leader. In the county authority where ostensibly there is no majority group, policy and resources is made up of one-third rank-and-file members. Appeal here would consist of letting the conflict between the two committees go before the council meeting.

Either way it does not appear that policy and resources committees make decisions which upset the political balances already achieved. The adjustments made are more reflective of maintaining control over resources and of using that control to hold education proposals within the fiscal tolerances chosen by the majority leadership. While minor changes may be made by policy and resources for presentation to the full council, the education committee is given the opportunity to reexamine and resubmit its requests. If there are political differences which persist, these are returned to the party group.

Council action follows an almost *pro forma* review in the party group. What the majority party has decided to pursue as a policy, what has been recommended by the education committee and that has been ratified by policy and resources moves predictably through the full council on the vote of the majority. The potential for upset is minimal, even in the rural county where there is no majority group to fix the directions. The next stage, implementation, puts the new policy in the hands of the officers for them to develop with the education committee.


## Implementation

There are two problems which chief education officers face as implementation begins. The first is to set about devising procedures and making consultative arrangements that are needed for operation of the policy. The second is to prevent political erosion of the policy by members either through modifications in application or through pleading of special cases. In both, he requires the help of the chairman to endorse his actions and to keep members in check. If the minority party strategy is to reduce the impact of the policy or if interest groups are determined to blunt it, the task is one of steering the chairman between operational flexibility and partisan inflexibility.

Officers work out the administrative procedures for

implementation. The directorate or office staff meeting is used to review the new regulations. Often there is consultation with advisors and teachers and with heads and governors to assure that the policy is understood in terms of its effects on schools. There may be adjustments to accommodate particular situations, but the chief education officer must approve them.

This is where erosion begins, according to officers. A member finds that several of his constituents are inconvenienced by the change or that there is a school in his ward which is going to be one of the last to receive benefit from the new policy. A governor, perhaps urged by a head, believes that the department used faulty figures in arriving at a solution for his school. Each situation has to be investigated and an answer provided. Some situations are unanticipated problems which require a modification. A high number of cases may indicate difficulty with the policy. Other situations seem to be presented as routine case work. Yet others bring real pressure for accommodation, and the chairman will have to be alerted for possible questions in committee. The most frequent seeking of exceptions reported were those related to allocation of secondary places. These authorities have lived with the problem long enough to develop careful regulations and appeal procedures. While councillors still try to obtain exceptions, committee chairmen have learned to leave it all to officers after the annual allocation policy has been adopted.

Some policies are implemented with advice from community groups, teachers and elected members in a round of consultations. There appears to be more and wider consultation in the county authorities than in the Outer London boroughs. Sectional matters, rural versus urban interests and greater necessity for variations are contributing factors. This implies the use both of *ad hoc* groups and of school or other organizations. In the boroughs, there is more use of existing associations and regularly constituted advisory groups such as joint consultative committees. At the same time, officers expressed the feeling that too much consultation was being demanded, thus taking officers away from other work.

To consult on how policy is to be implemented is a decision for the committee chairman and, perhaps, the committee. The usual tactic is to seek representation through *ad hoc* groups brought together for the purpose. This prevents established organizations from bringing excessive pressure to bear and from putting the authority in a position where it could be accused of playing one off against the other. The selection of participants is often based on officers' judgements about contributions to earlier rounds of consultation. An organization which was friendly to the policy proposal and which offered some reasonable ideas for its implementation is likely to be favoured. Teachers are selected on the advice of the joint consultative committee, while members are appointed by the chairman. In giving the minority representation, the shadow chairman or spokesman is usually asked for his nomination.

There are several purposes to such consultation. One is to inform and to let people know there is a new policy. Seeking support is another purpose, somewhat cooptive in nature, but designed to head off controversy by moving people to acceptance through participation. Third, there is a preventive aspect, the forestalling of complaints through explanation and the opportunity to question. The objective is to achieve some consensus on broad recommendations about how the policy might be operated, while finding out the pitfalls and sensitivities of its effects. The limited nature of the objective has led some interest group leaders to label this as less than genuine consultation. However, officers and members think it is sufficient to provide them with guidance.

As the results of consultation appear and as evidence is gathered on the effectiveness of regulations set by the department, the chief education officer begins to evaluate the policy. The chairman is kept informed as adjustments are made and as problems arise. When conditions change in schools and in the community, the chief seeks a possible policy revision and, perhaps, opportunity to initiate another policy change.

## Summary

The policy process for education from initiation to implementation emphasizes control of inputs and decisions. The series of decisions in the progression from professional response to political conclusion involves the chief education officer, the education committee chairman and the majority leader. The structure of the policy subsystem and party control are combined to make their interactions critical to the movement of questions from one stage to the next. Equally important are who decides what at each stage and the influence which the participants bring to bear on each other to condition what will occur at succeeding stages.

The complex set of activities related to bringing policy questions into the political arena is very important. The influence used here has the purpose of preventing political foreclosure of educational and service considerations. Through his hold on initiation, the chief education officer can negotiate the professional position and can ensure himself a central role in formulation of questions to be decided by the majority group.

The basis for policy is established through reformulation of opinion stage. Consent-building among members is carried out by the chief and the chairman. The strategy of using influence and how this task is divided can vary with the source of the issue, the degree of factionalism in the majority party or its need for allies, e.g. Independents, the disposition of the majority leader towards education and the personal style of the chief. The importance of this stage for development of support within the government can be seen by the fact that consultation outside the government is carefully limited and controlled.

Emergence of alternatives involves the balancing of professional proposals against party interests. The education committee structure is used to start the political resolution of questions. The main participant and dominant figure is the education committee chairman. His reference point, however, is the majority party group and party leadership, not the committee. The task is to keep committee recommendations within the framework established in earlier stages and approved by the group. Therefore, adjustments and realignments are made outside the committee at the interstices of the policy subsystem, the *ad hoc* chairmen's meetings and the presessions of the coordinating subcommittee.

Movement towards legitimization of the policy alternative chosen by the controlling party serves to place contentious items fully in the political realm. The party leader becomes dominant, supervising the political strategy designed to minimize dissent within his party and to blunt the opposition of the minority party. Advice is available from the chairman and the chief education officer in discussion and debate stage as they gather information through committee discussion and consultation with interest groups. Reference to organizations outside the government is made by consideration of the ability to control the use of results in line with general opinion of majority party policy. Before policy recommendations of the education committee are referred to the council, the leadership may modify or seek their reworking in terms of funding requirements through the policy and resources committee. This reflects the overriding concern of party leaders for demonstrating fiscal responsibility and use of financial controls as controls on council policy-making.

Further analysis and conclusions about the policy process and the participants will be developed in the final chapter. Some effects of party, both Labour and Conservative, will be noted. Projections about the politics of education in the near future will also be given.

# 7 Conclusions

The policy process for education in local authorities, examined through the perceptions of the main participants and others, consists of many interrelated decisions. Those who make the decisions, the politicians and professionals, interact in complex patterns of influence which shape the process. The structure of the policy subsystem for education as well as the constraints on decision-taking affect the participants and contribute to the purposes underlying their activities at each stage of the process from the initiation to the implementation.

This chapter presents conclusions about these points by looking first at the process itself. Next politicians and parties are considered in order to highlight particular characteristics which bear on the process. The chief education officer takes some risks when getting involved in politics and these are discussed in the conclusions about professionals. The final section, which deals with the public and policy-making, also provides a few indicators about future directions and some short-range predictions.

## About the Process

The policy process for education in local authorities takes place in an increasingly closed system which is characterized by an emphasis on domination and control through party political organization and direction. While there were variations in the degree of party domination and control in each of the six authorities studied, all showed evidence of having restricted and redefined the arena in which educational policy-making takes place. The autonomy of the local education authority as a government to devise its own internal processes has been used to limit access to the process by those outside the government and to regulate the interactions of those within the government. The controlling party overrides the committee system as the instrument for policy-making with the purpose of making the process more predictable by the prevention of a coalescence of forces which might generate other aims and alternative solutions to problems. Those forces would appear to include segments of the public, school governors, coopted members and teachers, as well as education officers and the minority party.

There are three aspects to this political enclosure of the process: to seize the extended structure for the governance of education, to define and use consultation in a manner which limits access and to make the party the vehicle for change through setting a pattern of control which confines initiation and response to those within the government at critical stages. All three aspects rest on the relative ease with which a cohesive disciplined majority can organize and dominate the structure of local government.

Those elements of the extended structure designed to provide for contribution and participation by people outside the government, coopted places and boards of governors, have been firmly enmeshed through the power of appointment and political choosing of those who serve. Teachers' organizations and interest groups have also been brought into the orbit of control through a combination of joint consultative bodies and cooptation, using or resting in part on ideological alignments with political parties. The degree of control differs depending on the political division of the council and the majority's willingness to exert control, but the basis is in the organization and the attempts to make coopted members and governing board seats into party positions. Where control cannot be exercised directly as with teachers' panels of consultative committees, the rules for interaction, made by those in government, effectively mitigate or neutralize those constraining forces by channelling participation. This domination of the extended structure was evident in all six authorities; it was virtually complete in the Outer London boroughs and was well underway in the counties.

As a result, the concept of the extended structure for educational governance has been turned inside out. Those elements

*183*

originally created to help to sense and to aid in solving local educational problems have been insulated by political domination. As with an insulated flask, external changes with the potential to affect what is going on inside penetrate at a controlled rate. Forces which might promote change, organizations and persons interested in local education, have become more part of the container than part of the contents.

Consultation as a means of promoting broad-based decision-taking, both inside and outside the government, has become subject to conditions which have the effect of limiting access to the policy process. Conditions stem from and revolve around assessments of power and influence by parties rather than evolve from expressions of interest and the need to know on the part of consultants. The results produce restrictions on who may be consulted and when. These restrictions, evident in all six authorities, tend to distort the meaning of consultation by *a priori* selection of those to be consulted and by delaying consultation until the political metes and bounds of decisions have been well established. Distortion becomes progressively greater as one goes from inside the government towards the community. This fulfils a political purpose in that it makes consultation amenable to control and the results more predictable.

Clearly, then, consultation has come to have multiple meanings applicable to different situations and, by inference, to different stages of the process. A lexicon of consultation is needed to know who is doing what with whom. There is 'genuine to-and-fro' consultation, i.e. exchanges of ideas and opinions to the point of agreement by a consensus to which all may contribute. It is consultation which is necessary and desirable and which takes place between equals or those who share responsibility, e.g. between the chairman and the chief education officer or between chairman and chairman. Consultation is also used to inform and to acquire information. It is an exchange between those who have the responsibility and those who might be in a position either to support or to block what is being proposed. The results may be used as each sees fit. This is necessary consultation that the chairman might take up with his council colleagues or with teachers' organizations. Another purpose of consultation is simply to gather opinions without any indication of how much consideration will be given to differences, leaving the decisions in the hands of those who sought the opinions. It takes place between those who have responsibility and those who do not. It is desirable consultation as between the committee and an interest group or the chief education officer and a school association. Whether it is participation or a palliative probably depends on the results as viewed by those consulted, but there is little doubt that those in the government keep their options open by the manner in which they put their questions.

The underlying factors are not difficult to find. Politicians see consultation as being of relatively little use within the system they have arranged for policy-making in education. It carries risks which clash with the notion of party responsibility to announce a programme and to press it through the council. Thus, the few who should be consulted are those who pose the least risk: council colleagues who need to be accommodated and friendly interest groups. Teachers' latent power presents a potentially higher risk, but that is diffused by conducting consultation through joint panels well within the system rather than with the separate teachers' unions.

Some different factors are behind officers' attitudes towards consultation, but they are not free of the restrictions imposed by political control. Within the government, it is a way of testing ideas and of looking towards a consensus. Within the community, it is a means of gathering opinions and of transmitting information. The study indicated that, while officers might want to do otherwise, they have had to adapt the use of consultation to internal struggles of politics and to accept greater stringency on its use for giving information and for gaining participation from those outside the government. Thus, the more critical it is for the chief education officer to build consent within the government, the more he must adhere to power and influence assessments as the basis for consultation.

The third aspect, setting a pattern of control, provides a reasonable division of labour under the hard shell of organization. Politicians control the process, while professionals contribute ideas and supervise their development. The party becomes a vehicle by which change can be brought about. Officers provide information and professional judgements. However, there is an exchange of role aspects which comes into operation. The exchange works, because it benefits everybody by making the system predictable. The normal concept of the policy process is one of narrowing choices about objectives, alternatives and means. Party political doctrines and resource constraints place wide parameters around choices at the outset. This places emphasis on the early stages of the policy process and is a factor which focuses on professional response.

The process throughout is characterized by a series of initiation and response situations among those within the government which transcends the strictures of the normative notion that elected members make the policy while officers execute it. The blurring of this distinction gives chief education officers the necessary freedom to carry out the political dimension of their role in matching professional views and party political desires. Members accept the exchange of role aspects as essential to the process, but they expect a reversion to more usual roles in discussion and debate and certainly before legitimization stage begins. Chief education officers for their part seem to be most punctual about reverting to the professional dimension of their role, although committee chairmen have access to their political observations.

Chief education officers generally like party political control because it lends predictability to policy-making. Once an idea is accepted by the majority, it is quite certain to be implemented. Some skilful handling is required, however, as the party vehicle is more like a juggernaut than a mini. What is to be sought and the resources which might be devoted to such ends are questions to which the chief requires early answers. This places an emphasis on his selling ideas, including those which modify majority party policy aims, in the initiation and reformulation of opinion stages of the process. Selling his ideas brings out the political dimension of his role.

The conditions of political control in an authority have an important bearing on the strategies of chief education officers. The strategies chosen appear to be those which minimize the risk to the chief while advancing his ideas. Clearly, the political dimension of his role grows out of his professional role. He cannot exceed nor jeopardize that basis by trying to bring the factions together or by getting commitments from members without at least the tacit approval of the chairman. 'Brokering' between parties is acceptable only after the majority has taken a direction in the group. Thus, the opinion-making activities of chief education officers were more evident in those authorities where the majority party was strongly organized and relatively free of factionalism and where there were close relationships between the chief and the majority leader. This was observed in the Conservative-dominated county, one of the Conservative-controlled London boroughs and to a lesser extent in the Labour-controlled borough. By contrast, chief education officers worked through their chairmen more in the other three LEAs: the rural county where there is no majority group, the Labour-controlled county which is riven with factionalism and the Conservative borough where a faction of 'strict Tories' has taken command and where the leader is not considered sympathetic to education. In the latter authority, the chief certainly displays some kind of political courage when he asks the minority leader to complain if the majority holds an item in the group.

The implication is that the chief education officer's political influence increases and that his risks decrease as the strength and cohesiveness of the majority party increases. This would appear to be exactly the result desired by both politician and professional if the process is to be kept predictable. At the same time, their interdependence provides some balance and keeps one from complete domination of the other. The particular style of a chief education officer plus the fact that he ought to emerge from the process with a policy that he and the department can administer may have an additional curbing influence on the party juggernaut.

One of the most observable effects of this enclosure of the policy process for education is that the identification and definition of problems and the reformulation of opinion about their meaning takes place almost entirely within the government. Indeed, nearly all opinion-gathering and opinion-making activities focus on members of the majority party. The modicum of external contributions to the statement of dissatisfactions and the crystallization of opinions are those suggested by the chief education officer in so far as he has been able to gather information and to arrange for consultation. The pattern of initiation and response ensures that the party group has a key role in determining whether the defined problem and the possible solutions are consonant with its broad aims in the government. The cumulative effect is most evident in the third stage of the process, the emergence of alternatives. The only policy solutions put forward for the consideration of the education committee are those that are proposed by the officers, with the approval of the committee chairman, and that are based in the aims and directions for education on which there is a consensus of the majority party group.

The result is a 'front-end loading' of the policy process by which the narrowing of choices is confined almost exclusively to professionals and politicians. The basis is that which the party can be expected to accept, while any expansion of this is that which the chief education officer can develop through opinion-making. These two factors limit the range of policy alternatives which can emerge. Once these decisions are made, relatively little change in policy direction takes place in succeeding stages. Paradoxically, it seems that the more strongly organized the majority party is, the greater the ability for the chief to use his political influence to expand the basis except possibly in issues where the political choices come first, e.g. on Department of Education and Science mandates or on issues known to be contentious between the parties. Expansion by the professional's use of politics can reduce the predictability of the process and this poses a question to which the chief must find an early answer—where is that upper limit?

Redefinition of the policy arena for education has other internal consequences for the process and for the participants. The most noticeable of these is an increasing inflexibility or rigidity in the framing of solutions to policy problems. The range of acceptable solutions is increasingly prescribed, and the spectrum of those contributing to solutions has been reduced. This rigidity arises because of party efforts at control and, because the process is becoming controlled, it is becoming more rigid. Careful regulation of consultation and limited give and take between parties are evidence of growing rigidity. It is easy to blame controlling parties for the situation, but evidence also points to acquiescence on the part of the minorities. They have agreed to and participated in making the extended structure political, they have the same ascending ladder of issue orientation from non-controversial non-partisan to party political by doctrine and dogma and they do not have a common cause with dissident community groups unless the dissent matches their own ideological inclinations. The party, Labour or Conservative *per se*, has little to do with this kind of inflexibility; both have displayed it in the authorities studied.

There are two reasons for rigidity. First, education has an

increasing importance as an area for local party policy-making and control. Parties no longer want to be in the situation of simply reacting when educational matters arise. As the changing context has provided opportunity for shaping education at the operating end of the system, parties have defined positions and have devised strategies for action. As soon as one party takes a position on an aspect of education, defines it in local terms and prepares to press its ideas in the council, flexibility is reduced. The trend may be more intense at this point in time, because the traditional autonomy of the education as a service area is being modified and because party leaders see their task as obtaining control of education while conditions are right. Second, resource constraints, particularly finances and the impact on the rates, are of overriding concern to party leaders. This is real, in so far as it is reflected in councillors' remarks about considerations they make in examining education proposals. Given an expensive service (and one which is also the largest of all local services), central government decrees which compel spending and a public which does not associate educational spending with rate increases, it seems that only the imposition of party responsibility on its policy-making is able to curb expenditures. Much of the control effort of the majority party is directed to this end through the checks applied in the coordinating subcommittee and in policy and resources.

Factors producing rigidity combine to make party leaders, especially majority party leaders, the precipitators of the trend in political control over education in local government. There is a general expectation that party leaders will weld together party aims and authority policies. This stems from their role as chief politician for the party and the powers they can wield through the policy and resources committee. The conditions which make educational policy-making more critical at the local level fall within that same expectation. The impact is made manifest in the actions of majority leaders.

It seems apparent from this study that majority leaders are actively seeking greater control over the policy process for education. The impetus is there, because failure to gain greater control creates the potential for the erosion of party cohesiveness and the onset of political repercussions. These points are evident from two impressions of leaders' outlooks on education.

The first impression is that majority leaders are biased against education in local government because of its intractability. The system with its separated structure is unwieldy. It requires a large amount of spending, which is not always readily amenable to authority control. Officers are considered expansionists with vested interests which they are good at protecting. Apart from that, committee chairmen become victims of officer domination, and members follow the chairmen because few of them have a real grasp of the immensity of the situation with which they are grappling. Education's huge appropriations make other chairmen jealous and harder to handle. In addition, there is often some segment of the public pressing the authority to do something for education.

The second impression is that party leaders have attempted to block off education at times, giving the service an expenditure limit and letting the committee do as it wishes within those funds; however, difficulty arises because, at other times, the leaders feel they need to have a hand in items such as the allocation of secondary school places, school sites and other issues. If these issues grow into controversy, it could be detrimental to the party, and the leader must respond because the responsibility for the political well-being of the party belongs to him.

What seems to be taking place as a consequence is a steady extension of leadership control into educational policy-making. Leaders and their group executive committees are increasingly vetting the proposals for education; committee chairmen are being instructed and are not permitted to hide behind the autonomy argument. Leaders, through policy and resources, are asking officers and chairmen to justify their requests, to explain how they account for results and to plan more prudently. The effects have already been noted: the setting of policy directions and a narrowing of the range of alternatives early in the process through the controlled pattern of initiation and response. The most important judgement for party leaders is to determine when control interferes with obtaining essential advice.

Enclosure and inflexibility are transforming the role of the education committee in policy-making. Discussion of substance and content within specified frameworks as determined by the leadership and the chairman mainly comprise the committee work where party domination is paramount. The results are the refinement of proposals as they progress through subcommittees into the main committee. The ability of the committee to influence process decisions is diminishing. The transformation is understandable in terms of process. It also seems to be acceptable to members in so far as they do not feel shut out when it comes to the contribution of suggestions and modifications to the substance of policy. Their real concern is that process decisions are beginning to interfere with decisions on content. This is evident in the ambiguities resulting from the introduction of policy and resources committees, particularly in those authorities where the leadership has begun to differentiate functions between it and the party group. While members can understand and cope with increased partisanship, it is disconcerting to feel a reduction in opportunities to exert political leverage within their own party.

The role of the education committee chairman appears to be undergoing subtle change, too. A reorientation away from the committee towards the leadership and the party group is the most evident change. While he remains an advocate for the service —its political defender and advisor—the chairman increasingly finds his reference point in the manipulative mechanisms of the system. He is no longer the chief politician for education but rather a facilitator in the conversion of educational ideas into policy. His task is to reduce the potential for conflict which could hinder the processs. The more important decisions which chairmen make and which they influence are process decisions which blend policy alternatives with political possibilities. This role aspect, often shared with the chief education officer, is evident in opinion-making activities, in gaining approval for proposals in the group, in keeping committee discussion focused on the alternatives presented and in defending his proposals before the policy and resources committee. It is also evident in the cutting off of extreme alternatives presented by the officers and in the channelling of items through the *ad hoc* meetings of subcommittee chairmen. These decisions are taken in the light of a group consensus which the chairman helped to develop, as well as because of the professional advice and political observations of the chief education officer.

How far the transformation of the committee and the reorientation of the chairman's roles will extend is difficult to predict. It has already been noted that the necessity for technical-professional understanding has reduced the role of the chairman. Greater control of the policy process fostered by the leadership both through the party and through the policy and resources committee is now adding to the squeeze on service committee prerogatives. The chairman as policy-maker is less prominent under these conditions. His role as facilitator is still being defined. What it will ultimately become depends mainly on the further definition of the relationship of chairmen to party leaders.

Overall, the reshaping of the policy process and changing roles of the participants that has come about through increased party domination benefits the controlling party in the way it governs the local education authority. The system for making decisions about education at the local level affords built-in protection from volatile community pressures and other forces. This provides the opportunity for consistent progress towards objectives in education through consistency of policies without disruptions brought on by unclarity and uncertainty of purpose. The system is predictable, so that the results of the process can be expected to provide solutions to problems that have been defined. Responsibility for the well-being of the service rests with elected officials and not with professional officers who do not have to face electors. It is the majority party which is identified with the results. At the same time, officers have an unmistakable focus for their technical and professional knowledge as well as for their efforts in the development of the service.

There are also benefits to the local education authority in its relationship to the central government, particularly the Department of Education and Science. The unpredictability of local education authority policy processes was identified as a source of mistrust between the two. The freedom of the authority to devise its own internal processes was considered a root cause of the problem. Under party control the policy process becomes predictable and, while the specific results may not meet Department of Education and Science expectations, they can demonstrate a consistency of political purpose. A concomitant result may be qualitative improvement in the ability of the local authority to explicate its difficulties in meeting Department of Education and Science requirements. Identification and definition of educational problems and objectives is made early in the process. They are subject to scrutiny because of their impact on authority resources and their effects on the educational system as the political implications are sorted out. Both of these factors, consistency of political purpose and the ability of the local education authority to state clearly its difficulties with mandates, have been demonstrated to be important in bargaining with the Department of Education and Science. Where new departures are being tried or where changing demands on the educational system of the nation provide some uncertainty about how things should be done, the local education authority under party control may retain more degrees of freedom in meeting Department of Education and Science requirements than an authority which is not.

The conclusions about the policy process itself have been presented. The next few sections present conclusions about politicians and parties, the place of the professional educator and the role of the public in the policy system. There are also a number of questions raised which require further study as part of the politics of education.

## About Politicians

The first question about politicians concerns the parties. Do the parties, Conservative and Labour *per se,* make a difference in the policy process for education? Certainly Labour has a longer list of doctrines and interests for education and also related areas such as equality of opportunity. There is also the continuing search for the socialist way of doing things. Conservatives, on the other hand, are more concerned about fiscal responsibility in the government and the preservation of a doctrine of least government. These points tend to form the philosophical boundaries for approaching policy-making but may be imperfectly reflected in the operation of the process. Where the party enters the picture, it is the strength and hardness of party organization that is critical. A well-disciplined majority with a tough leadership is much more likely to develop its aims early and to exert a greater degree of control over the process than one which has not coalesced for the purpose of legislation of a programme.

Labour appears to be harder and more unbending at times than do the Conservatives. This is often blamed on the concern for doctrine and dogma, an adherence to a socialist way of acting. More accurately, it arises because Labour tends to make political strategy decisions simultaneously with decisions on objectives. Behind this is the mutual interlocking obligation of the leadership and the committee chairman to carry out both decisions. In contrast, the Conservatives tend to reserve political decisions for the leader. This means that political strategy may not be devised until late in the process, e.g. if needed to gain legitimization of policy proposals. This might be a weakness for the minority to exploit in the absence of a clear direction within a Conservative majority, thus creating conditions for a 'stop, go' situation. However, the ability to adjust strategy could be a strength when the party is unified behind a set of aims. For example, curbing the excesses of partisanship particularly where a demonstration of responsive government might be preferable to riding roughshod over the opposition.

This difference in operation between Labour and Conservative parties also effects the chairman's facilitating role. Labour chairmen manage to make and influence more process decisions with their groups than do Conservative chairmen. Both the chairman and the party leadership are equally bound by such decisions in terms of both aims and political strategy. The Labour chairman then is less free to decide individually in the committee, but he has the backing of the leadership for decisions taken in the group to be applied in the committee. The Conservatives' split decision process means that, while chairmen are free to make decisions in and for committee operation, to be approved *post hoc* by the group, leaders may make political and, thereby, process decisions that are separate from the chairman's advice and, indeed, with prior sanction to do so from the group. Essentially, this makes the process initially indeterminate especially if a Conservative leader chooses to change the political strategy. Leadership control of the whip and the possibility that the strategy in policy and resources might well differ from that of the service committeeare further concomitants of a split decision process. The limitations on the chairman's facilitating role partially explains why the chief education officers in two Conservative-controlled authorities were quite assiduous in plying the majority leaders.

The party, Conservative or Labour, also has a bearing on whether or not the education chairman will be an influential politician within his party. The likelihood of having an influential chairman is apparently greater with Labour majorities. In part, this reflects Labour's concern for education as a service. It also reflects the internal promotion system of the party. Loyalty, hard work, accretion of personal power and recognition of one who can persuade others are attributes needed for gaining a prize chairmanship such as education. The Conservatives seem to prefer seniority and a streak of independence to personal power. These are useful in leading a committee but somewhat weak as qualifications for influence in a party.

The effect of having someone influential in the party as chairman has not been fully explored in this study, but it seems that chief education officers prefer an influential person as chairman. They did not detail what this might mean in terms of getting proposals through the process. Nevertheless, the way in which factions are brought together such as was accomplished by the chairman in the Labour-controlled county could be considered most helpful. An influential person might also be able to persuade the group towards a consensus faster and to emerge from the group with few adjustments to make in proposals. These points fit easily into the concept of the chairman as a facilitator but require further testing.

The importance of party groups in the policy process does not hinge so much on Labour or Conservative; it seems to depend more on the prevailing cohesiveness and discipline, on the quality of leadership and on whether the group is kept informed. A well-led group is more likely to have sorted out some directions and to be informed of what is coming up for decision. A poorly led poorly informed group in the majority can cripple or destroy committee proposals with amendments and special pleadings. It can also overreact with political strategies designed to 'cut the throats' of the opposition rather than simply to assure the passage of a policy. A group which is informed and whose leader sets the boundaries for decisions appears to approve what is proposed with relatively little difficulty, leaving it to the leader and the chairman to choose strategies for implementing the decisions of a consensus.

It must be said, however, that proper procedures and adherence to the ancient honourable rule of no surprises receives more emphasis in the groups than does the substance of the proposal. The opportunity for members to exercise the political prerogatives of group membership appears to be more prized than the decisions to be made through their exercise. This aspect is most evident in Labour groups and may partially explain why the chief education officers in the two Labour-controlled authorities took extra care and, indeed, extra steps in one to facilitate the translation of education proposals into politically feasible aims.

Another factor may afford a reason for the relative docility of majority groups in approving education proposals. That is undoubtedly the 'front-end loading' of the process wherein the chief education officer and the chairman through careful selection of ideas and much consent-building prepare the group and the leadership for what is coming. The question of costs appears to be settled early, thus meeting a central concern of party leaders. From there it becomes a matter of finding out individual discontents for mollification. The array of education subcommittees is used as a filter with the coordinating subcommittee, and the *ad hoc* chairman's sessions has the power to recycle questions in order to resolve conflicts. This does not guarantee that controversy will be avoided as the policy moves on towards implementation, but it does provide ample assurance of group consent and leadership endorsement.

This brings the discussion back to party leaders and their expectations for harnessing education within the local government. To some extent each leader that was observed followed his party in terms of purposes and methods for gaining ascendency over the policy process. In addition, each had his own concept of how far, how fast and in which style he should proceed. It is true that party leaders have power in the group which is reasonably commensurate with the responsibilities placed on them. However, achievement of a measure of control over the traditionally autonomous area of education as shown by several local education authorities in this study indicates nothing less than a superb mastery of internal party politics. While hardhandedness is an accepted means of pulling together the ideological ends and means of a Labour group, to impose discipline and a point of view on local Conservatives by the use of instruction and the whip is a distinct break with the past. Yet Conservative majority leaders in three of the authorities had little hesitancy in doing just that. The reactive thesis, the hardening of party discipline in one party and pressing the other into firmer partisan stances, is only a partial explanation.

A more critical factor, reflected in each authority, appears to be whether the members or the leaders will determine the way in which the policy and resources committee will be used. Whichever concept of policy and resources that a majority leader has, the Bains model or the party executive in government, he still has to be in command of it in order to ensure leadership and party control of the policy process. In order to implement his concept of policy and resources, a leader must be in command of his party group or, in the absence of a group, must fill committee seats with members sympathetic to his concept. The advent of policy and resources as a new and powerful political tool did much to precipitate the tougher style of party leadership which can be readily observed in the Outer London boroughs. It has grown quickly in the county authorities, too, but the way in which policy and resources will be used is not completely settled.

Although party leaders probably did not have education especially in mind when they seized on this political tool, the ability to control policy planning and finance are essential to harnessing education within local government. Certainly the financial aspect has been grasped through policy and resources. Obtaining greater control over policy planning is, as already noted, more difficult because political views underlie policy directions. This implies a need for a prior group consensus and those leaders adhering to the Bains model have to be sure that the consensus holds in the service committees. To be successful, a differentiation between policy and resources and the party group is essential. By filling committee seats with rank-and-file members and by confining political argumentation to the group, policy planning control can be achieved. While it is difficult to imagine a Labour chairman letting the leader remove him from the political prerogatives of group membership, Conservative leaders seem able, as they have in two authorities in this study, to make headway towards the differentiation.

The next section examines the risks to the professional as a politician and defines the limits of the chief education officer in the policy process.

## About Professionals

The chief education officer plays a key role in the policy process. How he perceives and conducts the political dimension of his role has far-reaching effects in each of the several stages. He has relative freedom to develop a style and to bring it to bear on political conditions as he finds them. Opinion-making is the critical task, and it is evident that chief education officers have recognized the changing locus of decision-taking from the committee and the chairman to the majority leader and the group as political control has advanced. However, with the change has come an increased need to make appropriate use of the professional basis which is central to the role of the chief education officer. The greatest danger lies in the temptation for the chief to sit with the party group or the group executive to promote the service and to make decisions about directions for education. The second greatest risk is in ignoring the fact that process decisions are subject to group examination and leadership manipulation.

It is assumed that each chief education officer knows the personal and career risks of going to majority group sessions should there be a sudden change in the electoral fortunes of the minority. The real risk is to his effective role in the process and to his purposes in developing the service. The temptation is there, because his participation can lend greater predictability to policy-making. The rationale is that the party leadership is going to make the decisions anyway. The rationale is, however, incomplete. Decisions are taken after advice and discussion, even in groups where the leaders introduce well-defined programmes to be put through the committee system. Participation in the group reduces the officers' opportunity for influencing others in the reformulation of opinion stage. If opinion-gathering is reduced, he loses the wider support that might exist for his ideas. If opinion-making is reduced, there is a reduction in the range of policy alternatives which can be presented. In other words, the officer is limited to those alternatives that he has agreed upon with the leaders. This may put short-term political decisions in the place of educational choices needed for the long-term development of the service.

The second risk is in ignoring the group's existence. The party is the vehicle for policy change, and it is the controlling party that takes responsibility for the policy chosen. While it might be appealing to have professional choices that are pure and simple, any councillor would point out that it is not the officers who have to face the electors. It is doubtful that there are many chief education officers who completely eschew use of internal politics, although some tend to rely on agreed recommendations in the education committee as a means of persuading the leadership.

This approach is managed through domination of the chairman or those of influence on the committee. Given a hardening party control and the fading of educations's traditional autonomy, the approach is increasingly inadequate. A strong chairman can help, but there is no substitute for a chief education officer who will take time 'to persuade the leader, to teach him and to explain some of the deliberations on education'.

Between these two high-risk situations there is reasonable variety in the ways that chief education officers bring their professional influence to bear on the process through the political dimension of their role. Judgements have to be made about the controlling party and its readiness to be persuaded. The purposes of party leaders have to be ascertained and, from these, determinations about how to capitalize on the facilitating role of the chairman and to utilize consultation as a political weapon when necessary.

A related problem for chief education officers is focused on the sharing of information about education in the authority. Minority members, coopted members, interest groups and some governors complain that they cannot obtain sufficient information from the education department in time, thus reducing their capability for contributing to decision-taking. The department is a centre from which the chief operates. His professional expertise is supported by its data-gathering and report-writing system. In itself, that is not surprising because such a far-flung multi-faceted service requires a well-organized information and communications network to focus on the problems requiring solution. What is amazing, however, is the degree of personal command exercised by the chief education officer, he supervises, directs and controls nearly every aspect of the department's work and all aspects of interaction with elected members. Apparently nothing goes to committees without his express approval, and no other professional officer in the department has a clearly defined and highly developed political role dimension. One purpose of his tightness of organization is to provide members with an unmistakable single professional voice. Because of the needs of his political role, this is appropriate. However, the concomitant effect is to assure a department monopoly on information and its dissemination. Controlling parties realize this and often place restrictions on sharing information with members of the minority and others. This is apparently causing some discomfort among chief education officers because it is too absolute, thus putting the 'gate-keeping' function somewhat ahead of his professional candour. The problem is how to relax the strictures on information without lessening the effectiveness of the department as a support centre for the necessary promotion of the service and without appearing to threaten the majority's ability to regulate the policy process.

The other professional educators concerned with the local education authority policy process are the teachers. The study described them as a constraining force to be reckoned with by policy-makers. The generalized objectives of teachers were reported, as were the different arrangements for their participation. Elected officials believed that they give generous consideration to teachers' views. What has not been shown clearly is whether teachers collect all of this together in order to persuade politicians and officers to move in particular directions. The potential appears to be there but evaporates at the edges of the policy process. Although further study is needed, the inference is that the arrangements for teachers' participation serve to neutralize teachers' power by dispersion of their interests and influence. The three meeting grounds provided by the local education authorities compartmentalize teachers' interests as employees, professionals and organization members. This is buttressed by authority control over the rules for selection and participation in joint consultation. Differences in outlook between unions and associations are probably used to advantage in this, e.g. the preference of the National Union of Teachers to pursue its ends quietly through cooperation with the government. This lends some credence to the National Association of Schoolmasters charge that joint consultative bodies are only talking-shops. None of this contributes to the creation of a single voice for teachers, and the drive to have only union and association representation in local authorities demonstrates that teachers' leaders recognize that there is a problem.

The final section raises some questions about another problem of participation, that of individuals and lay organizations concerned with education at the local level.

## About the Public and the Future

How members of the public perceive the policy process depends a great deal on their expectations from the government and on their interests in education. The process as it is operated provides a built-in protection from volatile outside pressures or it is insensitive to popular demands for change. Control by the majority party clearly indicates where responsibility lies or it can indicate another cause of insensitivity. The results will be consistent progress towards known objectives or they will demonstrate that the sources of ideas for change are carefully limited. This much is clear: the public perception of policy-making is fairly accurate. Decisions are taken in political context with little in the way of direct input by members of the public. The process advances through the first three stages, initiation, reformulation of opinion and emergence of alternatives, before wide consultation outside the government begins to raise specific questions with those who are interested and concerned about education. By then, the direction to be taken by the authority has been fairly well settled by the majority party. Consultation taken with the public may be classified as desirable and does not ask for opinions about establishing a policy but rather about how it will react to a policy which is being established.

The public picture shows some inaccuracies, too. Political polarization on issues does not take place early in the process, unless the matter is contentious between the parties. Such issues are only a fraction of the items which go before the education committee. What they observe is a majority party control as expressed in the aims and alternatives put up for action. As might be expected, few people note the number of policies adopted with the word 'agreed'.

Before turning to the problems of access to government and to greater citizen participation in raising educational questions, it is worthwhile to ask what the level of interest is in authority policy-making for education. Councillors recognize school associations and parent groups as relatively small and active in the affairs of the school but quite unconcerned about the entire school system. Interest group leaders confessed that they could not provoke any interest in authority problems. Officers and councillors alike said that there were individual complaints and cases but rarely any organized efforts to achieve change. Majority leaders did not see any connection between educational expenditures and complaints about the rates. No party leader believed that public dissastisfaction over education could lead to the defeat of the controlling party. Unless the public gets involved in a raging controversy such as going comprehensive, it has to be concluded that broad public interest in educational policies at the authority level is minimal.

For the citizen who shows little interest in participation, the ballot box provides a reasonable solution. A reading of each party's manifesto will reveal its intentions for education and, given the policy process as observed in these six authorities, if the party of his choice takes control, it is quite sure to move in those directions. That may sound simple, but the parties have told people many times that they mean what they say in their manifestos.

For those with a more active concern, the problem is more complex. A number of avenues have been effectively closed, and certain activities, while attention-getting, have lost their impact. Lobbying or descending *en masse* on the education committee is pointless: it acts at the legitimization stage, and the decision has already been taken. (One mass descent was observed during the course of the study. Compared with similar American experiences, it was so polite and civilized that one almost expected the chairman to invite everybody to stay on afterwards for a cup of tea!) Consultation or being consulted is useful but usually happens too late and in a limited form during the discussion and debate stage or at implementation. Interest groups and other members of the public have sought places on governing bodies as a means of asserting greater citizen input but as the study has shown, the politicians had got there first. It should also be said that, even with non-political majorities, the effect on the process would be negligible, because governors are not in a position to start a policy change. At their end of the system, they could only hope to mitigate the operation of a policy in a school or group of schools.

These organizations, especially interest groups, which seek appointments as coopted members may themselves contribute to party dominance. Cooptation, as a strategy for influence, is a two-way exchange if there is an equalization of power. Interest groups, by their own admission, do not have sufficient information, personnel, funds or influence with the electors to be considered powerful. Being articulate is not enough. On the other side, control of government machinery by a party gives it a more than ample power basis for interacting with outside organizations. Thus, for weak interest groups to gain seats for coopted members or places on governing bodies is a Pyrrhic victory which subjects them to the rules set for their participation by those in the government, enhancing party domination. By contrast, teachers' organizations have a power which is recognized through the arrangements made for their participation. Coopted places are given to teachers to fill as they choose, and the comments they make on proposals are accorded priority hearing by elected members.

The more effective strategies for concerned segments of the public should take advantage of the several stages in the process. The objective would be to contribute at emergence of alternatives stage. Some approximation of the chief education officer and his activities in the initiation and reformulation of opinion stages could be used. This would mean a change from the tactic of lobbying serially, i.e. starting with the chief education officer and then moving on to lobby elected members. Instead, both should be contacted simultaneously with the same message. The majority leader should receive attention at the same time. The purpose would be to have consultations that come under the heading of necessary, i.e. to inform and to be informed. This obviously means that recognition by the chief education officer is needed. Capture of a professional officer by interest groups is not feasible, but a sufficient number of cues from elected members and a nod from the chairman would provide a sound recommendation to the chief education officer.

In the near future, party political control is going to be paramount. This means that party leaders must be reached. Interested citizens might try gaining access through the advisory groups or working parties that provide recommendations to group executives. Some ideologically aligned organizations are already on these panels. It would be helpful for more 'objective' non-aligned associations to serve in this capacity. Political alignment is probably more of an advantage to the party than to the organization, and, if interest groups realize this, they might abandon alignment for more neutral stances, thus giving themselves a slight advantage as an organization with which the party or, even better, the parties should negotiate.

The difficulty for interest groups and interested citizens is that they lack a basis on which to build their power. Information is a department monopoly. Electors are more or less tied to party rather than to education. Teachers are using their power to seek their own ends with local officials, and there are no indications from this study that they want to share their power with others. Exploitation of sectionalism is self-defeating and not useful, because the politicians know how to handle that type of rebellion. In short, there seem to be few power levers to grasp.

The one consistent observation which councillors made about interest groups and about their potential for creating pressure in the policy process was that they are organized. This observation applied to the school unit level as well as to authority-wide federations. It was reflected in the publicity activities about which councillors complained. Ability to organize may be the power lever which can give interest groups greater access to the process. Combined with the growing political sophistication implied in councillors' observations, interest groups and their friends have continuing strength in school unit associations. These are respected by councillors and officers as is evidenced by their careful treatment. If ideological alignments are eliminated, interest groups could well affiliate more unit organizations to form the basis of authority-wide federations. Further organization is needed to draw attention to their contributions. This may be a matter of improving communication, and it may also reflect a need for building some interlocking obligations. At present, the units are not well coordinated for such tasks as changing governing structures. Making these changes is desirable if promotional activities already mentioned are to be successful, but some central authority-wide themes for action should be provided through federated structures.

It was remarked earlier that education issues to be debated in local authorities were those put up by a responsive and concerned public. It was also said that changing conditions call for new forces or the realignment of existing forces in the making of educational policy. This study has demonstrated that political parties at the local level are moving rapidly towards a domination of the policy-making process for education. This extension of control is partially in response to the unsettling controversies of the 1960s and partially an outgrowth of what party politicians perceive as imperative to the well-being of the political party. Given the essential freedom of the local education authority to regulate its internal policy processes, the changing conditions including local government reorganization and some redefinition of relationships between the Department of Education and Science and the local education authority, the political parties took the opportunity to do exactly what they exist to do—to organize and control policy-making in the government along lines of their own choosing. What the future holds for interested and concerned citizens is that, if they wish to be an effective force, it rests with them to find the means of realigning themselves in order to cope with the changed situation now that politicians and parties have made their moves.

# References

AGGER, R. E., GOLDRICH, D., and SWANSON, B., 1964, *The Rulers and the Ruled,* John Wiley, New York.

BARON, G., 1965, *Society, Schools and Progress in England,* Pergamon Press, Oxford.

—— 1968, 'Policy-Making and Local Education Authorities in England', paper presented at *Seminar on Educational Administration, University of New England, Armindale, Australia.*

BARON, G. and TAYLOR, W., 1969, *Educational Administration and the Social Sciences,* Athlone Press, London.

BATLEY, R., O'BRIEN, O., and PARRIS, H., 1970, *Going Comprehensive: Educational Policy-making in Two County Boroughs,* Routledge & Kegan Paul, London.

BEITH, A. J., 1972, 'Is There a Future for Non-Party Councillors?', *District Councils Review,* November, pp. 288-91.

BIRCH, A. H., 1959, *Small-Town Politics,* Oxford University Press, Oxford.

BIRLEY, D., 1970, *The Education Officer and His World,* Routledge & Kegan Paul, London.

BOADEN, N. T., 1970, 'Central Departments and Local Authorities: The Relationship Examined', *Political Studies,* no. 2, pp. 175-86.

—— 1971, *Urban Policy-Making,* Cambridge University Press, Cambridge.

BOADEN, N. T., and ALFORD, R. T., 1969, 'Sources of Diversity in English Local Government Decisions', *Public Administration,* Summer, pp. 203-24.

BRAND, J. A., 1962, 'The Implementation of the 1944 Education Act in Leicester: A Case Study in Administrative Relationships', Ph.D. Thesis, University of London.

*206*

—— 1965, 'Ministry Control and Local Autonomy in Education', *Political Quarterly*, no. 2, pp. 154-63.

—— 1974, *Local Government Reform in England*, Croom Helm, London.

BULPITT, J. G., 1967, *Party Politics in English Local Government*, Longmans, Green, London.

BURGESS, T., 1973, *A Guide to English Schools*, 3rd edition, Penguin Books, London.

BYRNE. E. M., 1973, 'Demand and Allocation of Resources in Secondary Education (1945-1965) in the Cities of Lincoln and Nottingham and the County of Northumberland', Ph.D. Thesis, University of London.

COLE, M., 1956, *Servant of the County*, Denis Dobson, London.

THE COMMITTEE ON THE MANAGEMENT OF LOCAL GOVERNMENT (The Maud Committee), 1967a, 'Report of the Committee', vol. 1 of *The Management of Local Government*, HMSO, London.

——, 1967b, 'Local Government Administration in England and Wales', vol. 5 of *The Management of Local Government*, HMSO, London.

THE CONSERVATIVE PARTY CENTRE, 1969, *Party Politics in Local Government*, The Centre, London.

COUSINS, P. F., 1973, 'Voluntary Organisations as Local Pressure Groups: Part I', *London Review of Public Administration*, part 3, pp. 22-30; 'Voluntary Organisations as Local Pressure Group: Part II', *London Review of Public Administration*, part 4, pp. 17-26.

COX, C. B., and DYSON, A. E. (eds.), 1971, *The Black Papers on Education*, Davis-Poynter, London.

DEARLOVE, J., 1973, *The Politics of Policy in Local Government*, Cambridge University Press, Cambridge.

THE DEPARTMENT OF EDUCATION AND SCIENCE, 1973, *The Educational System of England and Wales*, HMSO, London.

ECCLES, P. R., 1974, 'Secondary Reorganization in Tynemouth, 1962-1969', *Journal of Educational Administration History*, no. 1, pp. 35-45.

EDMONDS, E. L., 1965, 'Local Education Authorities and Teachers in England', *British Journal of Educational Studies*, no. 2, pp. 139-46.

—— 1969, 'Local Education Authorities: Present and Future', *Aspects of Education*, no. 9, pp. 46-57.

REFERENCES

EGGLESTON, S. J., 1966, 'Going Comprehensive', *New Society*, 22 December, pp. 944-6.

GLENNERSTER, H., and HOYLE, E., 1972, 'Educational Research and Education Policy', *Journal of Social Policy*, no. 3, pp. 193-212.

GREENWOOD, R., NORTON, A. L., and STEWART, J. D., 1969a, *Recent Reforms in the Management Structure of Local Authorities —The County Councils*, Occasional Paper No. 3, Series A, Institute of Local Government Studies, University of Birmingham, November.

—— 1969b, *Recent Reforms in the Management Structure of Local Authorities—The London Boroughs*, Occasional Paper No. 2, Series A, Institute of Local Government Studies, University of Birmingham.

—— 1970, *Recent Reforms in the Management Arrangements of County Boroughs in England and Wales*, Occasional Paper No. 1, Series A, Institute of Local Government Studies, Universities of Birmingham, January.

GREENWOOD, R., SMITH, A. D., and STEWART, J. D., 1971, *New Patterns of Local Government Organization*, Institute of Local Government Organization, Institute of Local Government Studies, University of Birmingham, August.

GRIFFITH, J. A. G., 1966, *Central Departments and Local Authorities*, Allen & Unwin, London.

—— 1969, 'Maud—Off the Target', *New Statesman*, 20 June, pp. 866-7.

HARTLEY, O. A., 1971, 'The Relations Between Central and Local Authorities', *Public Administration*, Winter, pp. 439-56.

—— 1972, 'Inspectorates in British Central Government', *Public Administration*, Winter, pp. 447-66.

HECLO, H. H., 1969, 'The Councillor's Job', *Public Administration*, Summer, pp. 185-202.

—— 1972, 'Policy Analysis', *British Journal of Political Science*, part 1, pp. 83-108.

THE INSTITUTE OF MUNICIPAL TREASURERS AND ACCOUNTANTS, 1973, *Education Statistics 1971-72*, The Institute, London, January.

—— 1974, *Education Statistics 1972-73*, The Institute, London, January.

JACKSON, P. W., 1970, *Local Government*, 2nd edition, Butterworths, London.

JENNINGS, R. E., 1975, 'Political Perspectives on Local Government Reorganisation,' *Local Government Studies*, October, pp. 21-37.

JONES, G. W., 1973, 'The Functions and Organization of Councillors', *Public Administration*, Summer, pp. 135-46.

KOERNER, J. D., 1968, *Reform in Education: England and the United States*, Weidenfeld and Nicolson, London.

KOGAN, M., 1971a, *The Politics of Education*, Penguin Books, London.

—— 1971b, *The Government of Education*, Citation Press, New York.

—— 1973, *County Hall: The Role of the Chief Education Officer*, Penguin Books, London.

KOGAN, M., and HERMAN, M., 1970, 'The Organization of a Local Education Authority: A Preliminary Analysis', unpublished paper, Brunel University.

THE LABOUR PARTY, 1967, *Local Government Handbook: England and Wales*, The Party, London.

LEE, J. M., 1963, *Social Leaders and Public Persons*, Oxford University Press, Oxford.

LEWIN, R. R., 1968, 'Secondary School Reorganisation in the Outer London Boroughs with Special Reference to the London Borough of Merton', M. A. Dissertation, Institute of Education, University of London.

THE LIBERAL PARTY, 1960, *Local Government Handbook*, The Party, London.

LOCKE, M., 1974, *Power and Politics in the School System*, Routledge & Kegan Paul, London.

MADDICK, H., and PRITCHARD, E. P., 1958, 'The Conventions of Local Authorities in the West Midlands: Part I', *Public Administration*, Summer, pp. 145-55.

—— 1959, 'The Conventions of Local Authorities in the West Midlands: Part II', *Public Administration*, Summer, pp. 135-43.

MANZER, R. A., 1970, *Teachers and Politics*, Manchester University Press, Manchester.

MILSTEIN, M. M., and JENNINGS. R. E., 1973, *Educational Policy-Making and the State Legislature: The New York Experience*, Praeger Publishers, New York.

NEWTON, K., 1973, 'Links between Leaders and Citizens via Local Political System', *Policy and Politics*, no. 4, pp. 287-305.

PESCHEK, D., and BRAND J. A., 1966, *Policies and Politics in*

REFERENCES

*Secondary Education: Case Studies in West Ham and Reading,* The London School of Economics and Political Science, London.

PETERSON, P. E., and KANTOR, P., 1970, 'Citizen Participation, Political Parties, and Democratic Theory: An Analysis of Local Politics in England,' paper presented at *66th Annual Meeting of the American Political Science Association, Los Angeles, California, September 8-12, 1970.*

THE RESEARCH UNIT ON SCHOOL MANAGEMENT AND LOCAL GOVERNMENT (THE ROYAL COMMISSION ON LOCAL GOVERNMENT IN ENGLAND), 1968, *School Management and Government,* Research Study no. 6, HMSO, London.

RHODES, R. A. W., 1975, 'The Changing Political-Management System of Local Government,' paper presented to the *ECPR London Joint Sessions, European Urbanism: Policy and Planning Workshop, London School of Economics and Political Science, April, 1975.*

ROBSON, W. A., 1968, *Local Government in Crisis,* 2nd edition, Allen & Unwin, London.

THE ROYAL COMMISSION ON LOCAL GOVERNMENT IN ENGLAND, 1969, vol. 1 of *Report, 1966-1969,* HMSO, London.

THE ROYAL INSTITUTE OF PUBLIC ADMINISTRATION, 1973, 'Creating the New Local Government', *RIPA Conference Report, 1973,* RIPA, London.

SARAN, R., 1967, 'Decision Making by a Local Education Authority', *Public Administration,* Winter, pp. 387-402.

—— 1973, *Policy-Making in Secondary Education: A Case Study,* Oxford University Press, Oxford.

SELF, P., 1971, 'Elected Representatives and Management in Local Authorities: An Alternative Analysis', *Public Administration,* Autumn, pp. 269-77.

SHARP, L. J., 1973, 'Theories and Values of Local Government', *Political Studies,* no. 2, 1973, pp. 153-74.

SMITH, W. O. L., 1971, *Government of Education,* revised edition, Penguin Books, London.

STEWART, J. D., 1972, 'Local Government: Changing Patterns of Management', *Education Management,* Supplement of *Education,* 23 June, pp. v-vi.

THE STUDY GROUP ON LOCAL AUTHORITY MANAGEMENT STRUCTURES (The Bains Committee), 1972, *The New Local Authorities: Management and Structure,* HMSO, London.

SUNDAY TIMES, 1974, 31 March.

SWAFFIELD, J. C., 1968, 'Local Government Changing', *New Society*, 19 September.

TURNBULL, J. W., 1969, 'Secondary Reorganisation in the London Borough of Croydon with Special Reference to the Role of Teachers' Organisations', M.A. Dissertation, Institute of Education, University of London.

URWIN, K., 1965, 'Formulating a Policy for Secondary Education in Croydon', in D.V. Donnison *et al.*, eds., *Social Policy and Administration*, Allen & Unwin, London, pp. 201–29.

VICKERS, G., 1973, 'Values, Norms and Policies', *Policy Sciences*, part 1, pp. 103–11.

—— 1974, 'Policy-Making in Local Government', *Local Government Studies*, February, pp. 5–11.

WISEMAN, H. V., 1963a, 'Local Government in Leeds: part I', *Public Administration*, Spring, pp. 51–69; 'Local Government in Leeds: Part II', *Public Administration*, Summer, pp. 137–55.

—— 1963b, 'The Party Caucus in Local Government', *New Society*, 31 October, pp. 9–10.

WOOD, C. A., 1973, 'Educational Policy in Bristol within the Context of National Educational Policy', M.Sc. Dissertation, Bristol University.

# Index